TRUMP PROMOTION

THE UPPERCUT

JAMES MARSH STERNBERG, MD (DR J)

authorHOUSE

AuthorHouse™
1663 Liberty Drive
Bloomington, IN 47403
www.authorhouse.com
Phone: 833-262-8899

Published by AuthorHouse 05/16/2022

ISBN: 978-1-6655-5952-2 (sc)
ISBN: 978-1-6655-5951-5 (e)

Print information available on the last page.

CONTENTS

PART I

PART II

ALSO BY JAMES MARSH STERNBERG

Playing to Trick One – No Mulligans in Bridge (2nd Ed)

Trump Suit Headaches; Rx for Declarers and Defenders

The Finesse; Only a Last Resort

Blocking and Unblocking

Shortness - A Key to Better Bidding (2nd Ed)

When Michaels Met The Unusual

From Zero to Three Hundred; A Bridge Journey

Reversing the Dummy

Trump Promotion; The Uppercut

James Sternberg With Danny Kleinman

Second Hand High; Third Hand Not So High
An Entry, An Entry, My Kingdom for an Entry
L O L; Loser on Loser
In Search of a Second Suit
Elimination and Endplay
Suit Preference; Abused and Misused

DEDICATION

To

CHRIS BALDWIN

The best tennis coach and my close friend. Thanks for all the hours trying to fix my volley.

ACKNOWLEDGEMENTS

This book would not have been possible without the help of several friends. Frank Stewart, Michael Lawrence, Anne Lund, Willie Fuchs, and the late Eddie Kantar, all provided suggestions for material for the book.

I am forever indebted to Hall of Famer Fred Hamilton and the late Allan Cokin and Bernie Chazen, without whose guidance and teaching I could not have achieved whatever success I have had in bridge.

My editor, and frequent co-author, Danny Kleinman, makes my writing better than it is.

And Vickie Lee Bader, whose love and patience helped guide me thru the many hours of this endeavor.

James Marsh Sternberg, MD
Palm Beach Gardens, FL
mmay001@aol.com

INTRODUCTION

How do defenders win trump tricks? Other than having high honors, natural winners, it's by getting a ruff of a short suit. Far more fulfilling and intriguing possibilities arise in poking away at declarer's trump suit and plucking out an unexpected trump trick. Trump promotion has been described as the magic of creating trump tricks that didn't exist at the beginning of the deal.

The basis for this is simple. Putting declarer in a position where to win the trick he must ruff high, thereby promoting one of the defenders' cards to a winner. At times this can be surprising and clever. Often when it seems you have no possibility of further defensive tricks, along comes a trump trick seemingly out of thin air.

A trump promotion, often referred to as an uppercut, creates a trump trick in a defender's hand where one didn't exist. This occurs mainly in two ways.

1. The lead of a plain suit card through declarer can allow partner to make an extra trump trick.
2. If a defender ruffs with a high trump, this may force declarer to overruff, thereby promoting a trump trick for that defender's partner.

Suppose the trump layout is as follows:

```
                N
    W         7 5 3         E
    J 9 4                 10 2
                S
            A K Q 8 2
```

Left on his own, South can draw trumps with no losers. But if West leads a suit of which both East and South are void, East should ruff high with the ten. Declarer has no winning option. If he discards, East has a trump trick. If South overruffs, West has a trump trick.

As a rule, declarer does best to discard a loser rather than get into a trump 'fight' and suffer a promotion. To thwart this, the defenders usually should try to arrange to cash their side suit winners before trying for a trump promotion.

A couple of actions to note involve giving a ruff/sluff where declarer has no losers to discard. But partner is also void and ruffs high enough to force the next hand, either dummy or declarer, to ruff with a relatively high trump.

GENERAL CONSIDERATIONS

What are some typical signposts to help recognize a deal as a candidate for an uppercut? There are no more side-suit winners for the defense. If there are, they must be cashed first. Otherwise, declarer can counter by discarding a side-suit loser rather than getting into a trump fight. You will end up just exchanging tricks.

You already know the advantage of playing after another player rather than before, especially when tenaces are held, like the KJ versus the AQ. This is also true when partner can play after the declarer in the trump suit.

A simple illustration:

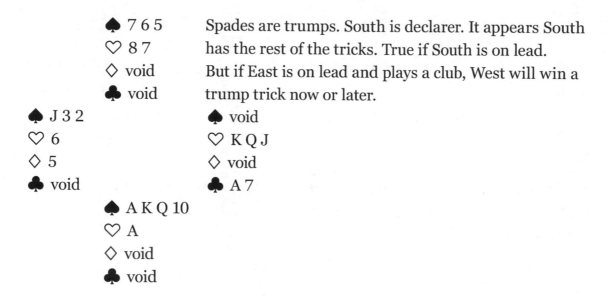

♠ 7 6 5   Spades are trumps. South is declarer. It appears South
♡ 8 7   has the rest of the tricks. True if South is on lead.
♢ void   But if East is on lead and plays a club, West will win a
♣ void   trump trick now or later.

♠ J 3 2   ♠ void
♡ 6   ♡ K Q J
♢ 5   ♢ void
♣ void   ♣ A 7

♠ A K Q 10
♡ A
♢ void
♣ void

Trump Promotion Plays

When partner has none of a suit, a trump promotion may be possible by leading that suit even if declarer or dummy also has none. Even if you give declarer a ruff/sluff, good things can happen as often declarer has nothing to sluff.

In the next few diagrams, you are looking at the trump suit. You are leading a suit in which partner has none and declarer is also forced to ruff.

(a)   North (dummy)

A K Q

West (YOU)   East

4   J 6 5

South

10 9 8 7 3 2

When North ruffs some other suit, East's jack becomes a trick.

(b)   North (dummy)

2

West   East (YOU)

9 6 4 3   J

South

A K Q 10 8 7 5

If East can ruff with the jack, South may overruff but that promotes West's nine to a trick.

(c)   North (dummy)

Q J 10 5

West   East (YOU)

8 3   K 9 2

South

A 7 6 4

If West ruffs with the eight, East has a trump trick. Also if West leads a suit for East and dummy to ruff, if dummy ruffs high, East can discard to promote his nine.

Forcing partner to ruff high often promotes trump tricks for yourself, the "uppercut", when both partner and declarer have none.

Observe these positions.

(d)   North (dummy)

7 5

West (YOU)   East

K 9 2   10 3

South

A Q J 8 6 4

When East ruffs with the ten, West now has two trump tricks after South overruffs.

(e)

	North (dummy)		
	void		
West (YOU)		East	
A 7 2		9 8 4	
	South		
	K Q J 10 6 5 3		

East ruffs with the eight, South overruffs. West wins the ace and gives East another ruff with the nine. West's seven is a third round winner.

Sometimes it's best to not rush to overruff declarer or dummy.

(f)

	North (dummy)		
	4		
West (YOU)		East	
Q 9 3 2		6 5	
	South		
	A K J 10 8 7		

When declarer ruffs with the jack, West gets one trick by overruffing, two tricks by not.

(g)

	North (dummy)		
	Q J 9		
West		East (YOU)	
2		K 10 8	
	South		
	A 7 6 5 4 3		

If dummy ruffs high, East gets two tricks by not overruffing, only one if he overruffs.

A similar situation: Spades are trump. A suit is led in which both South and West have none.

West		
♠ A 9 5 2	South	
	♠ K Q J 10	

If South ruffs with the king and West overruffs, South has the rest. If West does not overruff. West will score two tricks.

This is not always apparent. For example:

	J 5	
10 6 3 2		Q 9
	A K 8 7 4	

If South ruffs with the 7, West gains an immediate trick overruffing with the 10, but then South has the rest. By not overruffing, West scores two tricks.

Another layout:

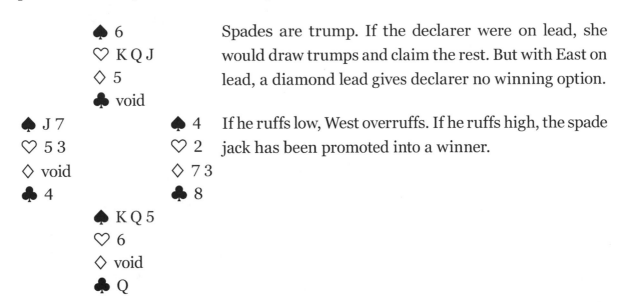

                 8 4 2
K 7 5 3   9 6   South ruffs with the 10. By refusing to
                 A Q J 10   overruff, West scores two tricks.

Another is when a defender has a holding almost but not quite good enough to
win a trick, frequently Qx or Jxx. This defender is the one seeking the uppercut while
partner is usually short in the trump suit.

♠ 6   Spades are trump. If the declarer were on lead, she
♡ K Q J   would draw trumps and claim the rest. But with East on
♢ 5   lead, a diamond lead gives declarer no winning option.
♣ void

♠ J 7   ♠ 4   If he ruffs low, West overruffs. If he ruffs high, the spade
♡ 5 3   ♡ 2   jack has been promoted into a winner.
♢ void   ♢ 7 3
♣ 4   ♣ 8

♠ K Q 5
♡ 6
♢ void
♣ Q

Sometimes a defender can obtain a trump promotion by refusing to overruff.

North
♠ A Q J 9   Spades are trump. Hearts are led by West or South.
♡ void   Knowing East has none, declarer must ruff high (queen
♢ void   or jack). If East overruffs, it's his last trick. If he discards,
♣ K   East   he now has K104 behind North's AQ9. East now has two
               ♠ K 10 4   tricks; the king which he was always getting, but also the
               ♡ void   ten – he can play low on the ace, take the queen with
               ♢ 8   king and the ten is now high, a second winner.
               ♣ 4

A simple example.

```
                ♠ 10 8 4
                ♡ A K J
                ♢ 10 9 7 3
                ♣ K 9 4
♠ A K Q 6 5 3              ♠ 9 7
♡ 7 6 3                   ♡ 10 8 4 2
♢ J 4                    ♢ Q 2
♣ 10 5                   ♣ 8 7 6 3 2
                ♠ J 2
                ♡ Q 9 5
                ♢ A K 8 6 5
                ♣ A Q J
```

Contract: 5♢ by South.
West leads the spade king and queen.
If West continues with a third top spade and East discards, declarer can ruff, draw trumps and claim.

But if West leads a low spade, and East realizes his ♢Q is a goner, he will ruff with the ♢Q. Declarer must overruff to avoid immediate defeat. Then West's ♢J will take the setting trick. Ruffing with the ♢2 would be futile. By taking care to lead a low spade instead of a third high spade, West guards against East discarding lazily and letting declarer ruff low.

West may not always be able to force partner to do the right thing.
For example:

```
                ♠ 5 3 2
                ♡ 7 6 5 2
                ♢ A J
                ♣ A K J 5
♠ K 10 4                  ♠ 9 8
♡ A K Q 10               ♡ J 4 3
♢ 9 5 4 3                ♢ 10 8 7 2
♣ 7 6                    ♣ 9 8 3 2
                ♠ A Q J 7 6
                ♡ 9 8
                ♢ K Q 6
                ♣ Q 10 4
```

Against 4♠, West leads the ♡AKQ, with South ruffing the third round. Declarer crosses to dummy with a diamond and loses a trump finesse to West's king.

With no side suit winners, the only hope to defeat the contract is a trump promotion. But West's last heart, the 10 is high.

Will East know to ruff West's winner?

Again, it's often best to leave nothing to chance. For example:

♠ A Q J
♡ 5
◇ K Q J 10 7
♣ A 7 5 3

♠ 3
♡ K Q 108632
◇ 9 5 3
♣ 9 6

♠ 10 9 7 4
♡ A 9 4
◇ 4 2
♣ J 10 8 2

♠ K 8 6 5 2
♡ J 7
◇ A 8 6
♣ K Q 4

North-South reach 6♠. West leads the ♡ King. If East plays an encouraging ♡9, will West continue hearts or consider the nine a signal for a shift to diamonds?

Best is for East to take over by playing the ♡A at Trick 1 and forcing dummy to ruff a heart. This play of forcing declarer to ruff with an honor is a common form of trump promotion. East now has a trump trick with his ♠10974.

LEARNING TO RUFF HIGH

♠ A Q 6
♡ Q 9
♢ Q 3
♣ K J 8 7 6 2

♠ J 10 8
♡ 10 4
♢ A 8 6
♣ A Q 5 4 3

♠ 9 5
♡ 8 5 3 2
♢ K J 10 9 7 4
♣ 9

♠ K 7 4 3 2
♡ A K J 7 6
♢ 5 2
♣ 10

South	West	North	East
1♠	P	2♣	3♢
3♡	4♢	4♠	All Pass

Opening Lead: ♢ Ace

West led the ♢A and continued a diamond to East's king. East returned the ♣9 to West's ace. West knows both East and South are now void in clubs. Is there any point in continuing clubs?

Here is the KEY play. West returns a middle club (actually any club). East must ruff with the ♠9, not the ♠5.

This promotes West's trump holding to the setting trick. Would you have known to ruff high? Here is the answer. Please write this down on your forehead for future reference.

You do not know South is going to overruff you. But you do know you are only getting one ruff. Does it matter to you which, the nine or the five? No, but JUST IN CASE a trump promotion is possible, ruff high. The nine will not have any other use. This is not difficult; it may be a surprising observation.

BUT – who knows how many times you may ruff high and nothing special happens. You win the trick, no one the wiser. Ruff high and win, ruff high and win, ruff high and win. And then one magic day you ruff high and it's a trump promotion! What a player you are! The kibitzers go crazy! Everyone asks, "how did you know to do that?" Take a bow!

A Serious Problem

Here is a situation I've seen too often and I'm sure you have too. You are trying to decide whether to lead back a suit thru declarer that both declarer and partner are void. You have the highest card in the suit, but dummy has the next highest.

A simple example would be dummy has Q 10 5 4 and you have K J 9 8 6. Partner led the ace and continued with the two, declarer follows to both tricks. Now what? Dummy has Q 10, you have K J 9. If you continue, (big if), high or low?

I went to the guru himself, Eddie Kantar, and found the 'answer' in one of his books, "Defensive Tips". Unfortunately, Kantar starts with "Are you ready for the longest tip in the book? If not, move right along."

The problem is if you lead high, you have established a winner in dummy. If you lead low, declarer can discard a loser. Are you still here with me? So what is Kantar's tip already? I'm going to quote (Eddie was a good friend; he told me it was OK).

First ask yourself these questions:
(A) How strong are partner's trumps?
   If Partner has worthless trumps, lead LOW
(B) Does dummy have any outside entries?
   If the idea is to kill an eventual ruffing finesse, lead LOW
(C) Does declarer have any outside losers?
   If dummy has no side entry, lead HIGH
(D) Can you cash your outside winners first?
   If the discard(s) will be of no value to declarer, lead HIGH
(E) Can you kill an eventual winner by leading low?
   If you need ONE trump promotion, cash your outside winners and lead anything
(F) Is it possible the suit should not be led at all?
   If you have a quick outside entry, lead HIGH; maybe a second trump promotion?
(G) How many more tricks do I need to set the contract?
   If you can't cash your outside winners and partner may have a natural trump trick, and there is a dummy entry, DO NOT LEAD THE SUIT AT ALL

**As Kantar wrote, "by now it doesn't matter, everyone has gone home."

Consider this deal:

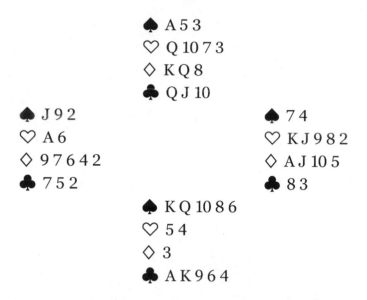

> ♠ A 5 3
> ♡ Q 10 7 3
> ◇ K Q 8
> ♣ Q J 10

♠ J 9 2   ♠ 7 4
♡ A 6   ♡ K J 9 8 2
◇ 9 7 6 4 2   ◇ A J 10 5
♣ 7 5 2   ♣ 8 3

> ♠ K Q 10 8 6
> ♡ 5 4
> ◇ 3
> ♣ A K 9 6 4

North opened 1♣ and East overcalled 1♡. South bid 1♠, showing at least a five-card suit. North rebid 1NT. When South next bid 3♣, North bid 4♠.

West led the ♡ Ace.

West continued a second heart to East's jack, declarer following.
How should East continue?

If East next leads a heart, high or low, declarer will succeed. After a high heart, declarer will ruff high, draw two rounds of trumps and discard the diamond loser on the heart queen.

After a low heart, declarer will take his discard immediately as West ruffs, trading tricks.

But if East cashes his outside winner, the diamond ace first, then any heart, high or low will defeat the contract.

This is an example of needing one trump promotion and cashing an outside winner, example of Kantar's (E).

Another example:

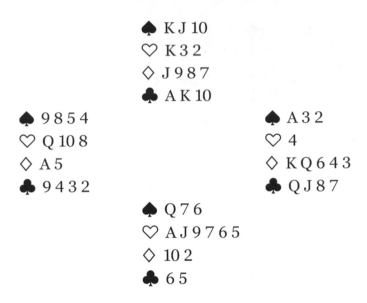

♠ K J 10
♡ K 3 2
♢ J 9 8 7
♣ A K 10

♠ 9 8 5 4
♡ Q 10 8
♢ A 5
♣ 9 4 3 2

♠ A 3 2
♡ 4
♢ K Q 6 4 3
♣ Q J 8 7

♠ Q 7 6
♡ A J 9 7 6 5
♢ 10 2
♣ 6 5

East opened 1♢ and South overcalled 2♡. North made one game try, bidding 3♢ but South signed off with 3♡.

West led the ♢ Ace.

West continued with a second diamond to East's queen, declarer following twice. How should East continue?

East cashed his outside spade winner, then continued with a high diamond. Was this successful?

Did East count his tricks? That was good for two diamonds, one spade and one heart. But where was the setting trick?

Declarer does not have a singleton spade. That would give West six spades and an ace. He never bid. Perhaps West can overruff twice? East needs to save his re-entry. Lead the ♢K. If West can overruff and put East on lead again, the contract will be defeated with a second overruff.

This is an example of Kantar's (F).

PART I

These deals show all four hands.
I suggest you cover the South hand and
your partner's hand until you have
decided how to defend.

DEAL # 1 LOOK WHO GREW UP

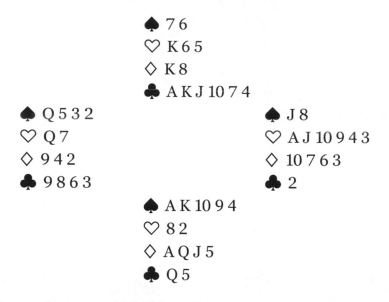

North opened 1♣, East overcalled 2♡, preemptive, and South bid 2♠. North bid 3♣ and when South bid 4◇, North bid 4♠.

West led the ♡ Queen.

The defense started with three rounds of hearts. Declarer ruffed the third round with the spade ten but West overruffed with the spade queen.

West returned a club. Declarer cashed the A-K of trumps. When the jack fell, declarer drew the last trump and claimed.

How could the defense have prevailed?

At Trick 3, instead of overruffing with a trick she was getting anyhow, West should discard a diamond. Declarer can next take the A-K of trumps, drawing East's jack but crashing the 7-6 in dummy.

Now West has the ♠ Q-5 behind declarer's ♠ 9-4. The spade five was going to be the setting trick. Maybe not what West envisioned when she first picked up her hand, the little ♠5 growing up to be the setting trick.

DEAL # 2 MAKE ONE UP

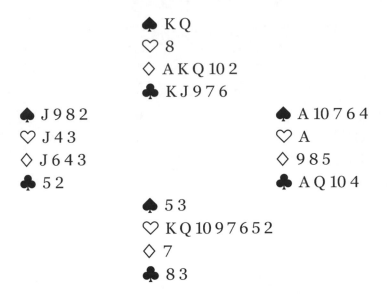

♠ K Q
♥ 8
♦ A K Q 10 2
♣ K J 9 7 6

♠ J 9 8 2   ♠ A 10 7 6 4
♥ J 4 3   ♥ A
♦ J 6 4 3   ♦ 9 8 5
♣ 5 2   ♣ A Q 10 4

♠ 5 3
♥ K Q 10 9 7 6 5 2
♦ 7
♣ 8 3

North opened 1♦ and East overcalled 1♠. South's 4♥ bid ended the auction. West led the ♠ 2.

East won the opening lead. Seeing three tricks, where was the fourth?

A spade ruff seemed unlikely, but he returned an unimaginative spade. Declarer lost three aces, making four hearts.

Too bad West hadn't led a club.

Could you have found a fourth trick?

Remember when there seems to be no hope, look to the trump suit, even though it might seem unlikely.

Seeing those diamonds, think ahead. Might there be a trump trick?

Cash the club ace and played another club. When in with the trump ace, play a third club and voila! Partner's jack of trumps is the setting trick!

He who looks finds.

DEAL # 3 WHOM TO TAP?

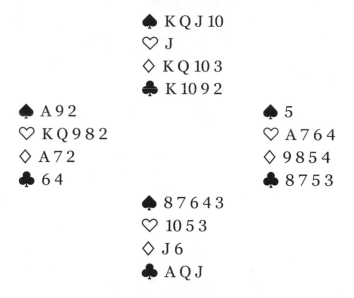

           ♠ K Q J 10
           ♡ J
           ◇ K Q 10 3
           ♣ K 10 9 2

♠ A 9 2   ♠ 5
♡ K Q 9 8 2   ♡ A 7 6 4
◇ A 7 2   ◇ 9 8 5 4
♣ 6 4   ♣ 8 7 5 3

           ♠ 8 7 6 4 3
           ♡ 10 5 3
           ◇ J 6
           ♣ A Q J

West opened 1♡. North made a take-out double. East bid 3♡, a weak jump raise. South bid 3♠ and North raised to 4♠. West led the ♡ King.

West held Trick 1. Picturing declarer needing to ruff, West switched to a low trump. Declarer won and played a diamond. West won and played two rounds of trumps.

Declarer had the rest, losing one spade, one heart, and one diamond.

What was the best defense? Was there another trick?

Usually shortening declarer's trumps is a good defensive ploy. and shortening dummy's trumps is counterproductive. But here West should see that if declarer ruffs twice in dummy, his ♠9 could be the setting trick.

West should see the obvious defense. Play another heart at Trick 2 making dummy ruff with an honor. West will be regaining the lead with an ace to make dummy ruff again.

Once dummy has used two honors, West's ♠9 will be the setting trick.

DEAL # 4 ANOTHER LITTLE GUY GROWS UP

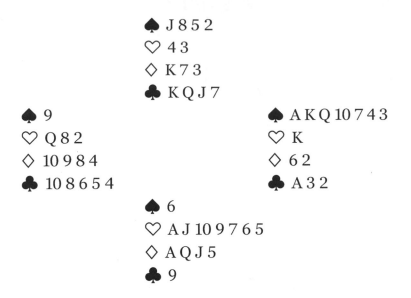

♠ J 8 5 2
♡ 4 3
♢ K 7 3
♣ K Q J 7

♠ 9
♡ Q 8 2
♢ 10 9 8 4
♣ 10 8 6 5 4

♠ A K Q 10 7 4 3
♡ K
♢ 6 2
♣ A 3 2

♠ 6
♡ A J 10 9 7 6 5
♢ A Q J 5
♣ 9

East opened 1♠ and South overcalled 2♡. North's 2NT was forward going. East persisted with 3♠ but South's 4♡ bid ended the auction.

West led the ♠ 9.

East won Trick 1 with the ♠10 and returned a suit preference ♠Q. Declarer ruffed with the jack of trumps and West overruffed with the queen. West returned a club and East led another spade.

Declarer ruffed with the heart ten and led the trump ace. When the king fell, the hand was over. Making four hearts.

How would you have defended? Should declarer go down one?

The defense can start the same, but when declarer ruffs with the heart jack at Trick 2, West should discard instead of ruffing with a natural trump trick. Declarer will lead the trump ace, dropping the king and continue with the ten.

East will win the queen and play a club to East's ace. When East now leads another high spade, the heart eight becomes the setting trick.

DEAL # 5 LITTLE THINGS MEAN A LOT

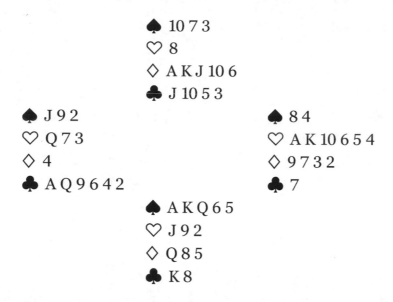

♠ 10 7 3
♡ 8
◇ A K J 10 6
♣ J 10 5 3

♠ J 9 2
♡ Q 7 3
◇ 4
♣ A Q 9 6 4 2

♠ 8 4
♡ A K 10 6 5 4
◇ 9 7 3 2
♣ 7

♠ A K Q 6 5
♡ J 9 2
◇ Q 8 5
♣ K 8

East opened a Weak 2♡ Bid. South overcalled 2♠. West bid 4♡ and North bid 4♠. West led the ♡ 3.

East won Trick 1 and made the obvious switch to his singleton club. Declarer played low, West won the club queen, then the ace, and continued with another club. East ruffed with the ♠4, declarer overruffed with the ♠5 and drew the trumps.
South discarded his heart losers on dummy's long diamonds and claimed.
Making four spades.

Who should be claiming, the offense or the defense?

The fate of the contract lies with East. He obviously is going to ruff the club, unaware South has no more clubs either.
You saw what happened when East ruffed with the four and declarer overruffed with the five. Declarer drew trumps and claimed.

But if East ruffs with the ♠8, look what happens! Declarer can overruff of course but with the ♠Q. Now West will be doing the claiming for down one, showing declarer his three trumps to the now high jack.
The key concept is East should realize his ♠8 is a goner anyhow.
How did you do?

DEAL # 6 WAMMO!

```
Dlr East              ♠ 7 5 4
Vul N/S               ♡ A 6 5 3
                      ◇ A K Q 5 2
                      ♣ 4
     ♠ A 9 2                         ♠ 10 3
     ♡ K Q J 10 8                    ♡ 4 2
     ◇ 10 6                          ◇ 9 8 4
     ♣ Q J 8                         ♣ A 10 9 5 3 2
                      ♠ K Q J 8 6
                      ♡ 9 7
                      ◇ J 7 3
                      ♣ K 7 6
```

East took advantage of the vulnerability and opened 3♣. South and West passed and North doubled. South bid 4♠. West led the ♡ King.

Declarer won the ace and led a spade to his king. West won the ace, cashed the ♡J and then led the ♡10. East discarded a club as declarer ruffed. Declarer drew the last trumps.

He scored four spades, one heart, and five diamonds.

OK, who are we going to blame this time?

Probably both East and West 50/50. Where is the extra trick coming from? Yes, of course the trump suit. West should make East ruff, high of course, by leading a heart other than the ten. West should lead the ♡8 on the third round of hearts.

If East ruffs with the ♠10, when South overruffs, West's nine has been promoted. If instead South discards, East cashes the club ace.

This is called an 'uppercut', forcing declarer to overruff to promote a trick for your partner.

DEAL # 7 SIMILAR UPPERCUTS

As in the previous deal, here are two more examples of possible layouts where an uppercut is possible. In both examples, spades are trump.

```
                    ♠ J 10 8 5
                    ♢ 4 3 2
   ♠ Q 4                          ♠ 9 2
   ♢ A K J 10 9 5                 ♢ 8 4
                    ♠ A K 7 6 3
                    ♢ Q 7
```

West leads the ♢AK. When West leads the ♦J, East needs to ruff with the ♠9.

Another example:

```
                    ♠ Q 8 5 4
                    ♢ 4 3 2
   ♠ J 9 2                        ♠ 10
   ♢ A K J 10 9 5                 ♢ 8 6
                    ♠ A K 7 6 3
                    ♢ Q 7
```

East needs to ruff the third diamond with the ♠10.

DEAL # 8 WIN OR DUCK?

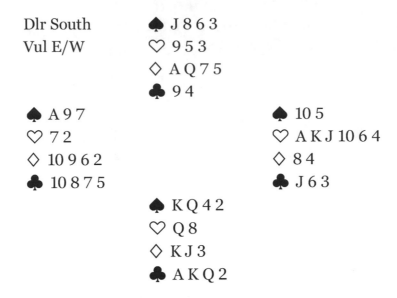

Dlr South
Vul E/W

♠ J 8 6 3
♡ 9 5 3
◇ A Q 7 5
♣ 9 4

♠ A 9 7
♡ 7 2
◇ 10 9 6 2
♣ 10 8 7 5

♠ 10 5
♡ A K J 10 6 4
◇ 8 4
♣ J 6 3

♠ K Q 4 2
♡ Q 8
◇ K J 3
♣ A K Q 2

South opened 2NT and reached 4♠ after a Stayman auction. Had the vulnerability been reversed, East might have ventured a heart overcall.

West led the ♡ 7.

East won Tricks 1 and 2 with the ♡AK and led a third high heart. Declarer ruffed with the ♠K and West overruffed with the ace. Declarer won the return, drew trumps and claimed.

Could you have found a killing defense?

Watch what happens if West does not overruff but discards. Declarer cannot avoid the loss of two trump tricks. If declarer leads the queen, West wins. Declarer has to lose a trick to the 9 or 10. If declarer leads low to the jack, West plays low and has the ♠A9 over declarer's remaining high honor.

Note that if West had started with doubleton ♠A9, he must overruff. Otherwise, declarer will duck the second round to his bare ace. If West now has bare ♠9 combined with East's ♠108x or 107x, the defense will win a second trump trick.

A good general principle: Overruff or uppercut with the short trumps, wait and discard with the long trumps.

DEAL # 9 ONCE MORE TO BE SURE

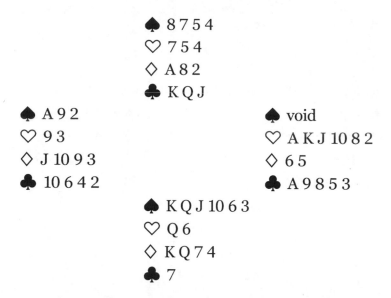

♠ 8 7 5 4
♥ 7 5 4
♦ A 8 2
♣ K Q J

♠ A 9 2
♥ 9 3
♦ J 10 9 3
♣ 10 6 4 2

♠ void
♥ A K J 10 8 2
♦ 6 5
♣ A 9 8 5 3

♠ K Q J 10 6 3
♥ Q 6
♦ K Q 7 4
♣ 7

East opened 1♡ and South overcalled 1♠. North cue bid 2♡ to show a good hand with spades. East bid 3♣ but South bid 4♠, ending the auction.

West led the ♡ 9.

East won the first two tricks with the ♡AK, declarer's queen dropping on the second round. East continued with the ♡10 and South ruffed with the ♠K.

How should West continue the defense? Let's compare two possibilities.

West overruffs with the ♠A and leads a club to East's ace. East plays another high heart. Declarer ruffs with the ♠10. Declarer has the ♠QJ6, West the ♠92. Declarer loses two hearts, one club, and one spade. Down one.

West does not overruff, but discards. Declarer has to draw trumps and leads the ♠Q. West wins the ace and plays a club to East's ace. East returns a high heart. Declarer has to ruff higher than West's nine. Declarer now remains with ♠J6, West with ♠92. A second trump trick for West. Down two.

Note a loser-on-loser play would let South hold the damage to down one. Instead of ruffing the third heart high, South can discard his singleton club.

East should cash the ♣A before continuing.

9

DEAL # 10 BASIC UPPERCUT

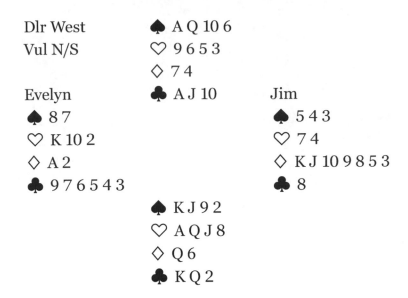

Dlr West   ♠ A Q 10 6
Vul N/S   ♡ 9 6 5 3
              ◇ 7 4

Evelyn   ♣ A J 10   Jim
♠ 8 7   ♠ 5 4 3
♡ K 10 2   ♡ 7 4
◇ A 2   ◇ K J 10 9 8 5 3
♣ 9 7 6 5 4 3   ♣ 8

           ♠ K J 9 2
           ♡ A Q J 8
           ◇ Q 6
           ♣ K Q 2

After two passes, East opened 3◇. South made a take-out double and North bid 4◇. South bid 4♡. West led the ◇ Ace.

At Trick 2, West continued with a second diamond, East winning the king. Seeing no future in the majors, East continued another diamond.

South really has no winning option. If South ruffs low, West overruffs with the ♡10 and later scores the ♡K. But what if declarer ruffs with the ♡J?
It depends if West is alert (and who West is). West was the infamous Evelyn.

South ruffed with the jack. Evelyn overruffed with the king. Declarer won the return, drew trumps and claimed.

"Evelyn, we just had a few hands like this, no?" I asked.

What if Evelyn had discarded anything instead of overruffing? Try not to overruff with a natural trump trick. Now with ♡K102 behind declarer's ♡AQ8, even Evelyn could probably take two tricks.

DEAL # 11 WHAT'S HE UP TO?

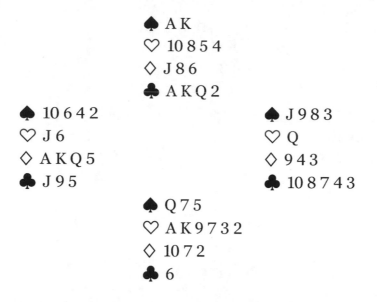

North raised South's Weak 2♡ Bid to 4♡. West led the ◇ Ace.

West continued with the ◇KQ as everyone followed suit.

How should West continue?

Much like the previous deal, there are no more outside tricks for the defenders. A trump trick? Perhaps.

West continued with the thirteenth diamond. Declarer discarded a club from dummy, and East?

How should East defend?

If East discards, declarer makes his contract. East should realize West had easy exit cards at Trick 4, a club or spade, and is offering declarer a ruff/sluff.

If East is awake and ruffs with the ♡Q, West's ♡J is the setting trick.

DEAL # 12 JIM CAN'T COUNT

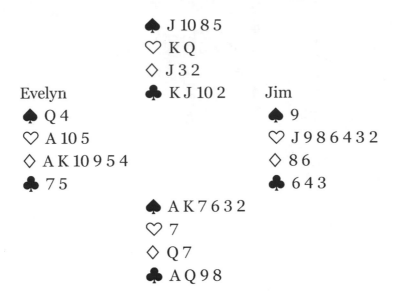

♠ J 10 8 5
♡ K Q
◇ J 3 2
♣ K J 10 2

Evelyn
♠ Q 4
♡ A 10 5
◇ A K 10 9 5 4
♣ 7 5

Jim
♠ 9
♡ J 9 8 6 4 3 2
◇ 8 6
♣ 6 4 3

♠ A K 7 6 3 2
♡ 7
◇ Q 7
♣ A Q 9 8

South opened 1♠ and West overcalled 2◇. North bid 3◇ showing a limit raise or better in spades with four card trump support. South bid 4♠.

West led the ◇ Ace.

Evelyn cashed the ◇AK at Tricks 1 and 2, then the ♡A, and led a club. Declarer won, drew trumps and had the rest.

Making four spades.

"Evelyn, you might have given me a diamond ruff," I suggested.

"No Jim," she replied. "Can't you count? Declarer was out of diamonds too."

There was no point in trying to argue with that. The fact that I had the one card to defeat the contract with an uppercut was not in Evelyn's bridge world.

The nine is a big card. Often with such a holding as Qx, and no other tricks on the horizon, a trump promotion may be your only hope despite the opponents having ten trumps.

DEAL # 13 ONE FOR MR. G

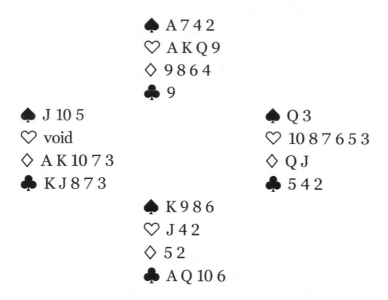

      ♠ A 7 4 2
      ♡ A K Q 9
      ♢ 9 8 6 4
      ♣ 9

♠ J 10 5   ♠ Q 3
♡ void   ♡ 10 8 7 6 5 3
♢ A K 10 7 3   ♢ Q J
♣ K J 8 7 3   ♣ 5 4 2

      ♠ K 9 8 6
      ♡ J 4 2
      ♢ 5 2
      ♣ A Q 10 6

West opened 1♢ and North made a take-out double. South jumped to 2♠ showing values and North bid 4♠. West led the ♢ Ace.

At Trick 1, East played the ♢Q. West knew East could win the second diamond so he led the ♢10. East won the jack and returned the ♡10. West ruffed but wondered why partner led the ♡10. Declarer had no diamonds either. West led a club.

Declarer won and drew trumps. Making four spades.

"Partner, my heart ten was suit preference, an attempt to get you to return a diamond rather than a club," said East.

East was correct. West should do as asked. If West plays another diamond, East will ruff high with the ♠Q. South can overruff, but now this UPPERCUT play promotes a trump trick for West's ♠J10 for the setting trick.

The term uppercut was first used by Charles Goren to describe a trump promotion. The French word "couper" means to cut, strike or a blow, and the French use this word to mean trump or ruff.

Goren added the pugilistic touch to describe this particular defensive play.

DEAL # 14 DESPERATE MEASURES

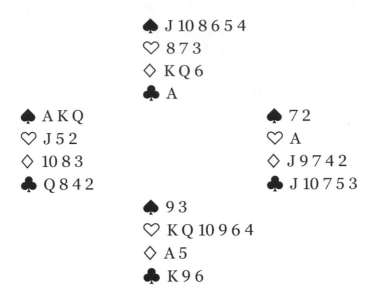

♠ J 10 8 6 5 4
♡ 8 7 3
◇ K Q 6
♣ A

♠ A K Q
♡ J 5 2
◇ 10 8 3
♣ Q 8 4 2

♠ 7 2
♡ A
◇ J 9 7 4 2
♣ J 10 7 5 3

♠ 9 3
♡ K Q 10 9 6 4
◇ A 5
♣ K 9 6

South opened 1♡. North bid spades, then raised hearts. South bid 4♡.
West led the ♠ Ace.

West continued with the ♠KQ. Declarer ruffed the third spade as East discarded.
She played a club to dummy and led a heart.

When East won the heart ace, the hand was over.

Could the defense have done better?

Yes. Trump promotions can be very obscure. If East counts his tricks, he can see
after the ♠AK, there are probably no other defensive tricks coming except trumps.

If East ruffs the spade queen with the ace of trumps, South goes down. A difficult
play. Too bad West didn't have a small spade to lead.

West's jack of hearts can be the setting trick.

DEAL # 15 ALONG SIMILAR LINES

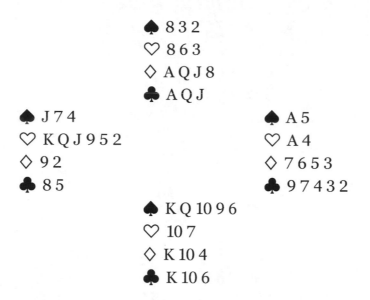

♠ 8 3 2
♡ 8 6 3
♢ A Q J 8
♣ A Q J

♠ J 7 4
♡ K Q J 9 5 2
♢ 9 2
♣ 8 5

♠ A 5
♡ A 4
♢ 7 6 5 3
♣ 9 7 4 3 2

♠ K Q 10 9 6
♡ 10 7
♢ K 10 4
♣ K 10 6

West opened 2♡, but North-South reached 4♠. West led the ♡ King.

East overtook the ♡K at Trick 1 and returned the ♡4. West won the ♡J at Trick 3 and persisted with a third heart. East discarded a club and declarer ruffed. South crossed to dummy with a club and led a spade.

Whether East ducked or won the first round of trumps, the defense was only taking one more trick.

Making four spades, losing two hearts and one spade.

Who was to blame? Could you have found another defensive trick?
What piece of information is missing above?

"When the shades of night are falling, look for the last glimmer of light." Here it's in the trump suit. What was the third heart that I didn't mention above?

If it was the ♡Q, blame West. If the ♡3, blame East. If East ruffs the third round of hearts with the ace of trumps, West scores a second trump trick for the defense. Yes. East could ruff the ♡Q with the ♠A but that's making life difficult for partner.

DEAL # 16 FANCY FOOTWORK

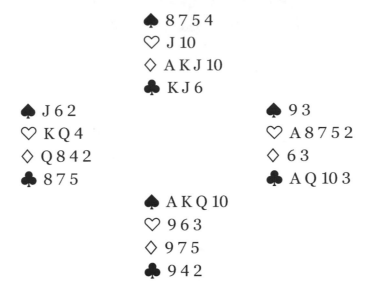

♠ 8 7 5 4
♡ J 10
♢ A K J 10
♣ K J 6

♠ J 6 2
♡ K Q 4
♢ Q 8 4 2
♣ 8 7 5

♠ 9 3
♡ A 8 7 5 2
♢ 6 3
♣ A Q 10 3

♠ A K Q 10
♡ 9 6 3
♢ 9 7 5
♣ 9 4 2

East opened 1♡, West bid 2♡ and North doubled for take-out. South bid 2♠ and everyone passed. Should E/W have carried on to 3♡?

West led the ♡ King.

East played an encouraging ♡8 at Trick 1. West cashed the ♡Q and switched to a club. East won two club tricks, but the defense was finished.

Declarer took the rest, with a winning diamond finesse.

An overtrick? How should East continue to defeat 2♠?

East should play a discouraging ♡2 at Trick 1. He needs a club shift now, not later. If West shifts to a club at Trick 2, East wins and plays a heart to West's queen.

Another club from West allows East to not only take two more club tricks, which would hold declarer to his contract, but by playing the thirteenth club, promotes a trump trick for West, the setting trick.

Down one. Hmmm, let's see, down one or an overtrick?

DEAL # 17 WHO IS TO BLAME?

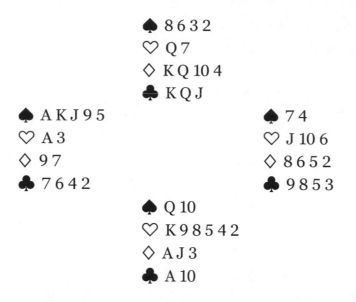

    ♠ 8 6 3 2
    ♡ Q 7
    ♦ K Q 10 4
    ♣ K Q J

♠ A K J 9 5   ♠ 7 4
♡ A 3   ♡ J 10 6
♦ 9 7   ♦ 8 6 5 2
♣ 7 6 4 2   ♣ 9 8 5 3

    ♠ Q 10
    ♡ K 9 8 5 4 2
    ♦ A J 3
    ♣ A 10

South opened 1♡, West bid 1♠, and North bid 2♦. When South rebid 2♡, North bid 4♡. West led the ♠ Ace.

West continued with the ♠KJ. East discarded a club at Trick 3 as South ruffed. Declarer played a trump to the queen and returned a trump. East followed with the ten and declarer ducked, losing to West's ace.

Declarer took the rest, making four hearts.

How could the defense have done better? Assign the blame.

How about 80% East, 20% West? Why?

East should ruff the third spade with the ♡10; it can't hurt and might help. South will overruff with the ♡K. But now when South leads a trump, West can rise with the ace and lead another spade. East's ♡J is the setting trick.

Why 20% West? Maybe West should force East to do the right thing by leading a low spade, not the jack, to force East to ruff, high we hope.
Hey, partners need help.

DEAL # 18 PROPERLY DEFENDED

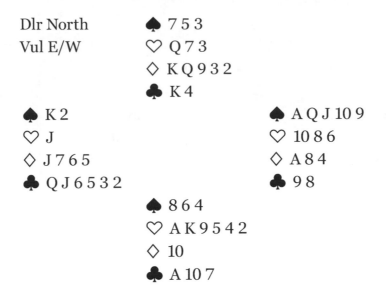

```
Dlr North        ♠ 7 5 3
Vul E/W          ♡ Q 7 3
                 ◇ K Q 9 3 2
                 ♣ K 4
♠ K 2                          ♠ A Q J 10 9
♡ J                            ♡ 10 8 6
◇ J 7 6 5                      ◇ A 8 4
♣ Q J 6 5 3 2                  ♣ 9 8
                 ♠ 8 6 4
                 ♡ A K 9 5 4 2
                 ◇ 10
                 ♣ A 10 7
```

After two passes, South opened A Weak 2♡ Bid and North raised to 3♡. Everyone passed and West led the ♠ King.

West led the spade king, then the spade two. At Trick 2, East won the nine, then cashed the spade ace. East then led another spade which would promote a trump trick for himself if West had even the heart jack.

Declarer was not looking for a trump fight. He simply discarded his diamond loser. The good news for East – he got the trump promotion. The bad news – East failed to defeat the contract.

How should East have defended?

East was careless leading another spade before cashing the diamond ace.
A basic rule of defensive play is cashing your side suit winners before trying for the trump promotion.

If East defends properly by cashing the diamond ace first, South has no counter. After the diamond ace and another spade, the heart jack promotes East's trump holding.
Down one.

DEAL # 19 A SIMILAR SITUATION

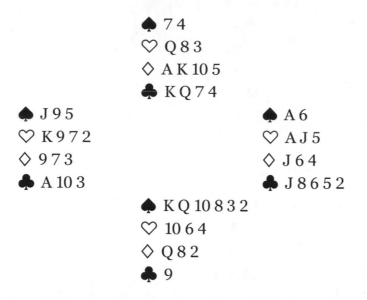

♠ 7 4
♥ Q 8 3
♦ A K 10 5
♣ K Q 7 4

♠ J 9 5   ♠ A 6
♥ K 9 7 2   ♥ A J 5
♦ 9 7 3   ♦ J 6 4
♣ A 10 3   ♣ J 8 6 5 2

♠ K Q 10 8 3 2
♥ 10 6 4
♦ Q 8 2
♣ 9

North opened 1♣ and rebid 1NT after South's 1♠ response. South's 2♠ rebid ended the auction. West led the ♥ 2.

East won Trick 1 with the ♥J. East cashed the ♥A and returned his last heart to West's ♥K. West played the thirteenth heart for East to ruff with the ♠A promoting West's ♠J, potentially into the setting trick.

But declarer claimed, "Making two spades."

Huh? How did that happen?

The first three tricks were fine. But West overlooked a crucial play in seeking a trump promotion – cash your side winner first. At Trick 4, as East ruffed high, declarer had discarded his club loser.

West must cash the club ace first, otherwise declarer can throw a loser.

Now the thirteenth heart allows the defenders to enjoy their trump promotion.

DEAL # 20 FALSE COUNT

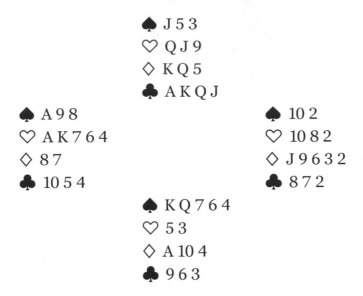

North opened 1♣ and rebid 2NT, 18 − 19 HCP, after South responded 1♠.

South bid 3◇, artificial and forcing, asking for more description of North's major suit holdings. When North showed three spades, South bid 4♠.

West led the ♡ Ace.

East played the heart deuce at Trick 1 giving count, the attitude being known. West switched to a diamond and declarer claimed ten tricks, losing one spade and two hearts.

Was there another trick available for the defenders?

Perhaps. Suppose East plays the ♡10 at Trick 1. West will continue with the ♡K and a third heart expecting East to ruff. When East follows, West may be temporarily annoyed, but patience is a virtue.

When declarer leads a spade to the king, West can win the ace and play yet another heart. East will ruff with the ten of spades. When declarer overruffs, West has a second trump trick.

"Nice play of the heart ten," West begrudgingly said to her husband.
"Just trying to help steer you in the right direction, dear."

DEAL # 21 WATCH THE SPOTS

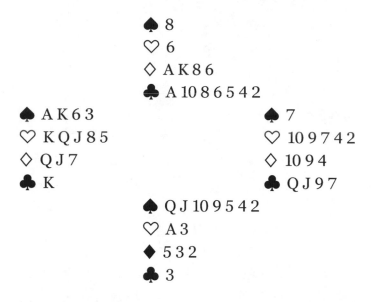

```
                        ♠ 8
                        ♡ 6
                        ◇ A K 8 6
                        ♣ A 10 8 6 5 4 2
  ♠ A K 6 3                              ♠ 7
  ♡ K Q J 8 5                            ♡ 10 9 7 4 2
  ◇ Q J 7                                ◇ 10 9 4
  ♣ K                                    ♣ Q J 9 7
                        ♠ Q J 10 9 5 4 2
                        ♡ A 3
                        ◆ 5 3 2
                        ♣ 3
```

West opened 1♡ and North overcalled 2♣. East's preemptive jump to 4♡ did not stop South from bidding 4♠. West doubled, ending the auction.

West led the ♡ King.

Declarer won the ace and ruffed a heart (maybe I should have led a trump, thought West?) Declarer played the club ace and ruffed a club with the spade queen.

How should West continue the defense?

Please don't tell me you overruffed. A good rule is only overruff with useless trumps, not tricks you were getting anyhow. Watch.

If you overruffed, declarer will be able to draw trumps, losing one more trump trick. Making four spades doubled, losing two spades and one diamond.

If you discarded, watch the spots. West still has ♠ AK63. Declarer has ♠ J109542. South's jack loses to your ace. His ten loses to your king. His nine takes your three. But now_____ your six is higher than his five!

Could declarer have played in a different manner? Not your problem.

DEAL # 22 SEEK AND YE SHALL FIND

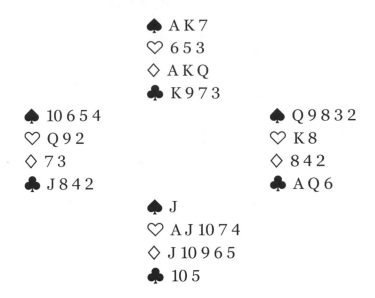

North opened 1♣ and rebid 2NT, 18-19 HCP after South had bid 1♡. South bid 3◇, New Minor, asking for more description about North's majors. North showed three-card heart support and South bid 4♡. West led the ♣ 2.

East won the first trick with the ♣Q. East counted her tricks; two likely clubs, maybe one heart. She made a passive diamond return. Declarer lost a trump finesse to West's ♡Q, who led a second club. East won and played another diamond. Declarer continued trumps.

When the ♡K fell, declarer claimed.

Was there a more successful line of defense?

As usual, when there are no more obvious tricks, look to the trump suit. At Trick 2, East can cash the ♣A and play a third club. Declarer can take a trump finesse losing to the queen.

Now another club from West allows East to ruff with the ♡K, overruffed by declarer's ace.

But now West's ♡92 behind declarer's ♡107 is the setting trick.

DEAL # 23 HIGH AS YOU CAN

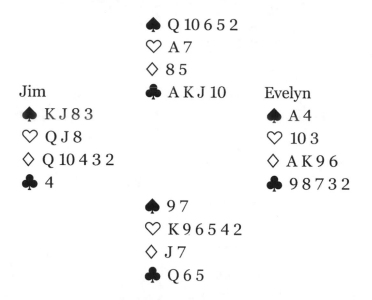

North
♠ Q 10 6 5 2
♡ A 7
◇ 8 5
♣ A K J 10

Jim
♠ K J 8 3
♡ Q J 8
◇ Q 10 4 3 2
♣ 4

Evelyn
♠ A 4
♡ 10 3
◇ A K 9 6
♣ 9 8 7 3 2

South
♠ 9 7
♡ K 9 6 5 4 2
◇ J 7
♣ Q 6 5

North opened 1♠, South bid 1NT, forcing for one round. North rebid 2♣ and South bid 2♡ ending the auction. West led the ◇3.

East cashed the ◇AK, West followed with the queen at Trick 2 on the off-chance Evelyn was watching. It seemed unlikely West started with a doubleton; that would give South five clubs and six hearts.

Yes. Evelyn was watching. What a girl! She cashed the ♠A and seeing Jim's encouraging ♠8, she continued with the ♠4. Jim won the ♠K and led the ♠3.

Evelyn, taking her life in her hands, ruffed with the ♡3. Declarer overruffed with the ♡4.

Declarer made 2♡, losing two spades, two diamonds, and one heart.

How could the defense have prevailed?

At Trick 5, East needs to ruff with the highest heart she can, the ten. The defense has run out of side tricks so it's time to see about some trump tricks. The ten does the job. It beats the contract whenever West has as little as QJ8 and saves an overtrick when West has as little as J92.

Declarer will have to overruff with the king and now West has two trump tricks instead of one. Down one.

DEAL # 24 LISTEN TO THE BIDDING

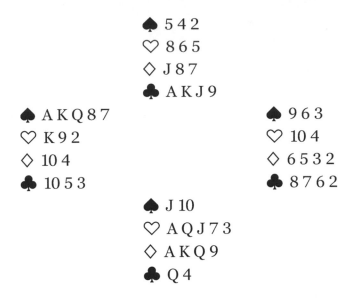

♠ 5 4 2
♡ 8 6 5
♢ J 8 7
♣ A K J 9

♠ A K Q 8 7
♡ K 9 2
♢ 10 4
♣ 10 5 3

♠ 9 6 3
♡ 10 4
♢ 6 5 3 2
♣ 8 7 6 2

♠ J 10
♡ A Q J 7 3
♢ A K Q 9
♣ Q 4

West opened 1♠ and, right or wrong, was followed by two passes to South who doubled. North bid 2♣. South bid 2♡, North raised and South bid 4♡.

West led the ♠ Ace.

West continued spades. South ruffed the third round of spades. He went to dummy with a diamond and took a losing heart finesse (What a surprise). West led another spade, East ruffed with the heart ten.

South overruffed but West now had another trump trick, the ♡92 behind the ♡A7. Down one.

"Partner, where were you during the bidding?" asked North.

South set himself up for failure. The heart finesse was a waste of time and gave the defense a chance to do what it did. With only twelve missing high cards, who do you think has the heart king?

With West's opening bid and East's pass, just lead the ♡A, then ♡J. When both opponent's follow, claim.

DEAL # 25 DECLARE OR DEFEND?

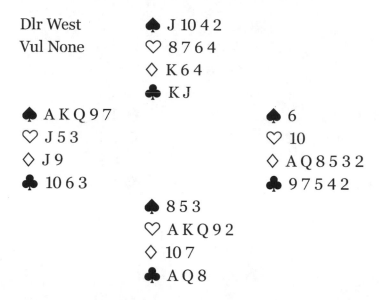

Dlr West   ♠ J 10 4 2
Vul None   ♡ 8 7 6 4
              ♢ K 6 4
              ♣ K J

♠ A K Q 9 7   ♠ 6
♡ J 5 3   ♡ 10
♢ J 9   ♢ A Q 8 5 3 2
♣ 10 6 3   ♣ 9 7 5 4 2

             ♠ 8 5 3
             ♡ A K Q 9 2
             ♢ 10 7
             ♣ A Q 8

After three passes, South opened 1♡. West overcalled 1♠ and North bid 2♡. Everyone passed. West led the ♠ Ace.

West continued with the ♠KQ. East followed once, then played the eight and five of diamonds. West played a fourth spade, East ruffed with the heart ten. Declarer overruffed and turned eight tricks into seven.

West's heart jack became the setting trick.

Which did you chose, declare or defend?

South can always succeed against this defense. He knows the diamond ace is offside. West is a passed hand. Instead of overruffing he should discard a diamond, protecting his eight tricks, five hearts and three clubs.

But West, instead of the fourth spade can still get his own trump promotion. East was begging for a diamond switch.

If West switches to the jack of diamonds at Trick 4, three rounds of diamonds and declarer is helpless to prevent a trump promotion in West's hand. The winner is---------defend.

DEAL # 26 WHOOPS

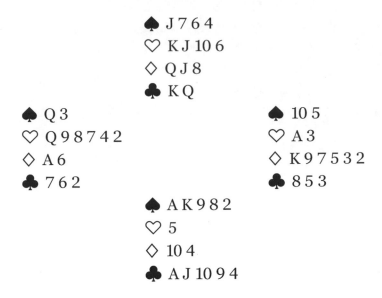

♠ J 7 6 4
♥ K J 10 6
♦ Q J 8
♣ K Q

♠ Q 3
♥ Q 9 8 7 4 2
♦ A 6
♣ 7 6 2

♠ 10 5
♥ A 3
♦ K 9 7 5 3 2
♣ 8 5 3

♠ A K 9 8 2
♥ 5
♦ 10 4
♣ A J 10 9 4

South opened 1♠ and despite West's skinny 2♥ overcall became declarer in 4♠. West led the ♦Ace.

West encouraged with the ♦9. West played a second diamond. East won the king and played a third diamond, promoting East's ♠Q.

That was the good news. The bad news was declarer was soon claiming, making four spades.

Whoops, what happened?

East forgot Bridge 101. In his excitement to promote a trump trick, he forgot Bridge Principle # 1 from Bridge 101.

Be sure to cash outside high winners first. South had discarded his heart loser at Trick 3, not wanting to get into a trump fight.

If East cashes the ♥A first, the contract is down one. So easy in retrospect, so easy to mess up in the heat of battle.

DEAL # 27 NO, NO, NO

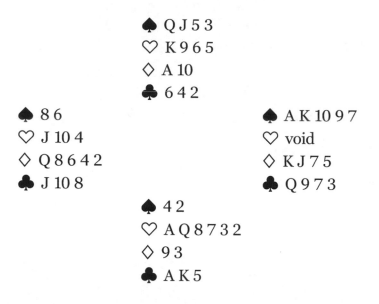

♠ Q J 5 3
♡ K 9 6 5
◇ A 10
♣ 6 4 2

♠ 8 6
♡ J 10 4
◇ Q 8 6 4 2
♣ J 10 8

♠ A K 10 9 7
♡ void
◇ K J 7 5
♣ Q 9 7 3

♠ 4 2
♡ A Q 8 7 3 2
◇ 9 3
♣ A K 5

East opened 1♠. South overcalled 2♡ and North raised to 4♡.
West led the ♠ 8.

At Trick 1, declarer played the ♠J from dummy and East won the ♠K.

East continued with the ♠A and led the ♠10. Declarer ruffed with the ♡Q and led the ♡A.

When East showed out, declarer had to lose a trump trick. One minor loser could be discarded on the spade queen, but he still had four losers: two spades, one trump, and one minor. Down one.

Who played worse, East or South?

I'd flunk both of them. If East wins the first spade and switches to a club, South is just going down. His play violated Kantar's Rule G: Don't try for the trump promotion when it will set up winners in dummy if you can't cash your outside winners first.

South failed to take advantage of East's blunder. Instead of ruffing, he can simply discard one minor loser. He ends up losing two spades and a spade ruff, but no minor losers since the other is later discarded on the high spade.

Painful to watch. You will recall this topic was discussed under a Serious Problem earlier, with a list of Kantar's suggestions.

DEAL # 28 DIRECTING THE DEFENSE

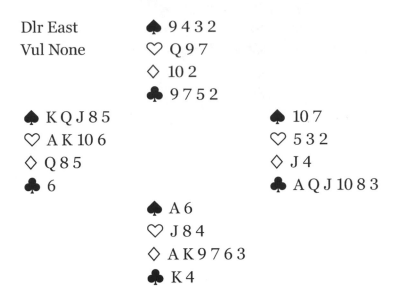

Dlr East
Vul None

♠ 9 4 3 2
♡ Q 9 7
♢ 10 2
♣ 9 7 5 2

♠ K Q J 8 5
♡ A K 10 6
♢ Q 8 5
♣ 6

♠ 10 7
♡ 5 3 2
♢ J 4
♣ A Q J 10 8 3

♠ A 6
♡ J 8 4
♢ A K 9 7 6 3
♣ K 4

In a team game, East opened 3♣ and South overcalled 3♢. Smelling blood, West doubled and led the ♡ Ace.

At Trick 1, East played a discouraging deuce. West switched to the ♠K. Declarer won, drew two rounds of trumps and forced his way to dummy in hearts. He led a club. Down one, losing one spade, two hearts, one diamond, and one club, for minus 100.

When East/West compared, their teammates were minus 300. Why?

West was correct that there was no rush to shift to a club. The other West at Trick 2 cashed the ♡K and played a third heart. In dummy for the only time, declarer led a club. East won the ace and returned a suit preference club three.

West ruffed and played the thirteenth heart. East ruffed with the ♢J. South discarded a spade loser, but another club from East promoted the ♢Q for West.

If East had two small diamonds, she would have returned a middle club. The club three, a suit preference card, called for the trump promotion play.

DEAL # 29 RUFF/SLUFF AWAY

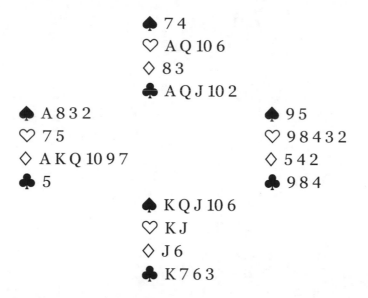

```
              ♠ 7 4
              ♡ A Q 10 6
              ◇ 8 3
              ♣ A Q J 10 2
♠ A 8 3 2                    ♠ 9 5
♡ 7 5                       ♡ 9 8 4 3 2
◇ A K Q 10 9 7              ◇ 5 4 2
♣ 5                        ♣ 9 8 4
              ♠ K Q J 10 6
              ♡ K J
              ◇ J 6
              ♣ K 7 6 3
```

South opened 1♠ and West overcalled 2◇. North bid 3♣, game forcing, knowing the heart suit would not get lost. South would bid hearts if he had four or more. When South raised clubs, North bid 4♠. West led the ◇Ace.

West continued the ◇K as East played the ◇2 then the ◇4. Not wanting to give declarer a ruff/sluff, West shifted to a heart. Declarer knocked out the ace of trumps and claimed.

Was there another trick somewhere for the defense?

A ruff/sluff is only a problem if declarer has something to sluff. West could account for all the HCP. He can let declarer sluff away.

If West plays a third diamond at Trick 3, declarer wins and starts the trumps. West wins the spade ace and plays another diamond, another ruff/sluff.

But when East ruffs with the ♠9, West's ♠8 is the setting trick.

DEAL # 30 NOTHING ELSE, SO

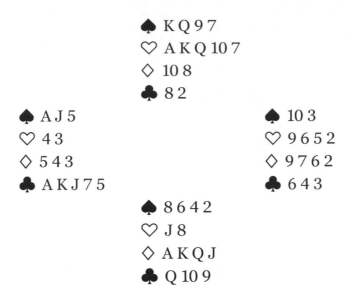

♠ K Q 9 7
♥ A K Q 10 7
♦ 10 8
♣ 8 2

♠ A J 5
♥ 4 3
♦ 5 4 3
♣ A K J 7 5

♠ 10 3
♥ 9 6 5 2
♦ 9 7 6 2
♣ 6 4 3

♠ 8 6 4 2
♥ J 8
♦ A K Q J
♣ Q 10 9

North opened 1♥ and South bid 1♠. Anemic spades, but hey, both partners can't have the AKQ. When North raised spades, South bid 4♠.

West led the ♣ Ace.

At Trick 1, East played the ♣3. West continued with the club king. East played the six and West played a third club.

Declarer won and led a trump. West played the ♠A and led another club, promoting a trump trick for the defense.

If declarer ruffed with the nine, East would overruff. If he ruffed with an honor, West had ♠J5 and East ♠10.

This deal was reported some years ago in the ACBL Bulletin by Eric Kokish.

Who was West? My friend and frequent teammate, Alan Sontag, one of the all-time greats, a real gentleman and a credit to the game.

DEAL # 31 IN THE RIGHT ORDER

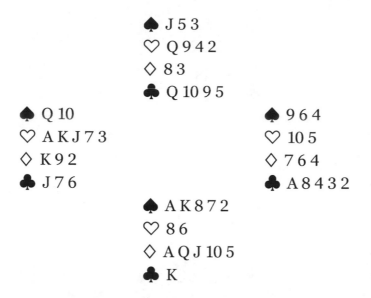

♠ J 5 3
♡ Q 9 4 2
◇ 8 3
♣ Q 10 9 5

♠ Q 10
♡ A K J 7 3
◇ K 9 2
♣ J 7 6

♠ 9 6 4
♡ 10 5
◇ 7 6 4
♣ A 8 4 3 2

♠ A K 8 7 2
♡ 8 6
◇ A Q J 10 5
♣ K

South opened 1♠. West overcalled 2♡. After two passes, South bid 3◇ and North corrected to 3♠, ending the auction. West led the ♡ Ace.

West could count three, possible four tricks. Where was a fifth? At Trick 1, East played the ♡10. West continued with the ♡K, then another heart ruffed by East with the ♠9, promoting West's queen. But declarer discarded his club loser.

Making three spades, losing two hearts, one diamond, and one spade.

How could the defense accomplish everything that was needed?

Better timing. If South was void in clubs, there was probably no defense. But West should lead a club at Trick 2. East wins the ♣A and plays a heart back to West. Now the third heart creates the trump promotion and declarer has nothing to discard.

Down one, the same losers as above plus one club loser.

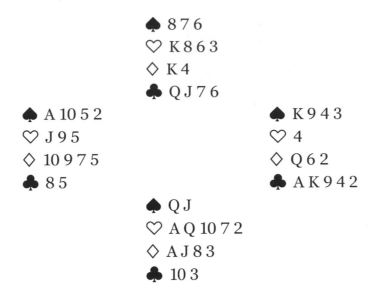

    ♠ 8 7 6
    ♡ K 8 6 3
    ◇ K 4
    ♣ Q J 7 6

♠ A 10 5 2   ♠ K 9 4 3
♡ J 9 5   ♡ 4
◇ 10 9 7 5   ◇ Q 6 2
♣ 8 5   ♣ A K 9 4 2

    ♠ Q J
    ♡ A Q 10 7 2
    ◇ A J 8 3
    ♣ 10 3

South opened 1♡. North bid 3♣, an artificial 2♡ raise, single raise values but with four trumps. East doubled. South bid 3♡ ending the auction.

West led the ♣ 8.

East won Trick 1 with the ♣K, cashed the ♣A and played a third round. Declarer discarded a spade as West ruffed. But the best the defenders could do now was cash one spade trick.

Declarer made three hearts, losing two clubs, one spade, and one heart.

How should we assess the blame?

Give East a speeding ticket. He was in too much of a hurry to give West a ruff. There were two, not just one, outside tricks that needed to be cashed first. Also East could see that a third club would set up the clubs in dummy.

At Trick 2, East should shift to the ♠3. West will win and return a spade. After East wins the second spade, now it's time for the trump promotion.

This is an example of Kantar's #E; cashing all outside winners, then leading anything since setting up the dummy's clubs by then won't help declarer.

Was East's double lead directing? Perhaps, but I like to play that double of a single raise bid is take-out, double of a limit raise bid is lead directing. Note East-West can make a number of spades. East was a little light for his take-out.

DEAL # 33 THREE DUCKS IN A ROW

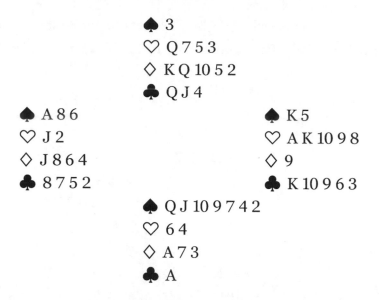

♠ 3
♥ Q 7 5 3
♦ K Q 10 5 2
♣ Q J 4

♠ A 8 6
♥ J 2
♦ J 8 6 4
♣ 8 7 5 2

♠ K 5
♥ A K 10 9 8
♦ 9
♣ K 10 9 6 3

♠ Q J 10 9 7 4 2
♥ 6 4
♦ A 7 3
♣ A

South opened 1♠, North bid 1NT, forcing for one round. East overcalled 2♥ and South rebid 2♠. After two passes East persisted with 3♣.

South's 3♠ bid ended the auction. West led the ♥ Jack.

The ♥J held Trick 1 as East played an encouraging ten. West continued with the ♥2, East winning the ♥8 as South followed. East continued with a high heart and declarer ruffed with the ♠9. Quack (duck) number one.

Declarer leads the ♠Q. Hurdle number two. Are you winning this trick? No? Good. Quack number two. East won the ♠K and played another high heart. Declarer ruffed with the ♠10. E tu? Quack number three!

Finally, you have ♠A8 and what does declarer have? ♠J7. Guess who is taking two more tricks now, mister!

Notice if at any time you had taken a spade trick earlier, you would have won only one trump trick, not two.

Patience is a virtue.

DEAL # 34 WHO'S IS UPPERCUTTING WHOM?

Declare or defend? You can pick; 4♡ by East or 4♠ by South. South opens 1♠, North bids 1NT, East bids 4♡. Pass and defend or bid 4♠ and declare?

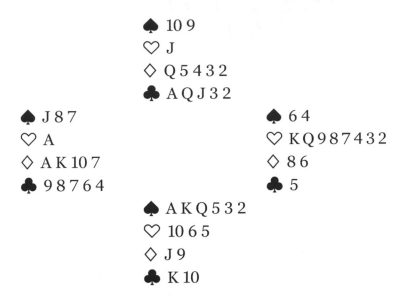

You want to bid 4♠ and declare? OK, West cashes the ♡A, the ◇AK, and then leads the ◇7. Now what? What's the 'magic' card?

You (West) need partner to have, and trump the ◇7 with the ♠6, not the ♠4. This promotes a trump trick for you. A very nice uppercut!

OK, want to declare 4♡? Let's say South passes after the 4♡ call.

South leads the ♠AK as everyone follows. South cashes the ♣K, the key play to prevent a loser-on-loser play when South next leads a third spade.

Partner also has a 'magic' card, the ♡J. This will promote a trump trick for South. Another nice uppercut!

But wait! North has overtaken the ♣K with the ♣A. Is she East's relative? East ruffs the ♣Q return and leads to dummy's ♡A. Whoops...stuck in Lodi. One way or another, it's South who will uppercut with the ♡10. Down one.

Which did you choose? Declare or defend? Everybody's getting uppercut.

DEAL # 35 GETTING HIT RIGHT AND LEFT

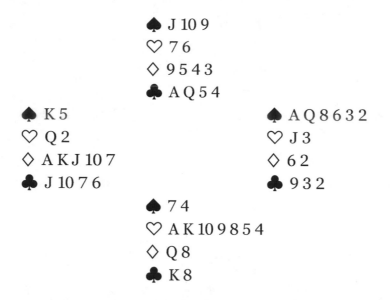

♠ J 10 9
♡ 7 6
◇ 9 5 4 3
♣ A Q 5 4

♠ K 5
♡ Q 2
◇ A K J 10 7
♣ J 10 7 6

♠ A Q 8 6 3 2
♡ J 3
◇ 6 2
♣ 9 3 2

♠ 7 4
♡ A K 10 9 8 5 4
◇ Q 8
♣ K 8

East opened a Weak 2♠ Bid and South's 3♡ overcall ended the auction. West led the ◇ Ace.

At Trick 1 East correctly played the ◇6, starting a high-low as declarer falsecarded, dropping the ◇Q. West trusted East to have played the ◇2 if she had started with ◇862. So West continued with the ◇K and then the ◇J. East made a valiant effort to save the defense by ruffing West's winner with the ♡J, promoting a trump trick for West.

But declarer threw a loser-on-loser ♠4. That was the third trick declarer lost and the ♠A was his fourth. He made 3♡, losing two diamonds, one heart, and one spade.

What basic principle did West overlook to cause this tragedy?

Cash winners first. Two ways to beat 3♡. West can lead the ♠ 5 at Trick 3. East will win and return a spade. Now the ♡J uppercut will be successful.

Better is to lead the ♠K to Trick 3. East can overtake with the ♠A, cash the ♠Q and lead a third spade. West scores the ♡Q with an overruff.

Or before cashing the second diamond, West can play the spades, then cash the other high diamond and let East ruff a diamond with the ♡J.

Poor South! Uppercut or overruff. Punches from both sides. Painful.

DEAL # 36 YOU'RE NOT FINESSING ME

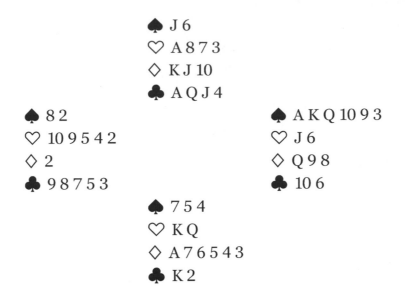

```
                    ♠ J 6
                    ♡ A 8 7 3
                    ◇ K J 10
                    ♣ A Q J 4
        ♠ 8 2                      ♠ A K Q 10 9 3
        ♡ 10 9 5 4 2              ♡ J 6
        ◇ 2                        ◇ Q 9 8
        ♣ 9 8 7 5 3              ♣ 10 6
                    ♠ 7 5 4
                    ♡ K Q
                    ◇ A 7 6 5 4 3
                    ♣ K 2
```

East opened 1♠ and South overcalled 2◇. North cue bid 2♠, a good hand with diamonds. East passed (double here should say don't lead my suit, an SOS double, "Some Other Suit") and South bid 3◇. With neither partner having a spade stopper, North-South landed in 5◇. West led the ♠ 8.

East won the first two tricks. Since West was certainly not overruffing the dummy, East switched to a heart. Declarer counted the HCP. East needed the ◇Q for his opening bid. With a trump finesse, he took the rest of the tricks. Making five diamonds.

Could East have defended differently?

West said, "If you play another spade, I'll ruff with the ◇2 and win an award for the lowest card to provide a trump promotion." Was she right?

No. East should have done it himself. East knows his partner is not taking any tricks on power. And his trump queen is precariously placed. But with his good diamond spots, a trump promotion is possible.

If East continues a third high spade at Trick 3 forcing dummy to ruff with the ◇10, East is assured of the setting trick.

DEAL # 37 SHORTNESS IS A DETRIMENT

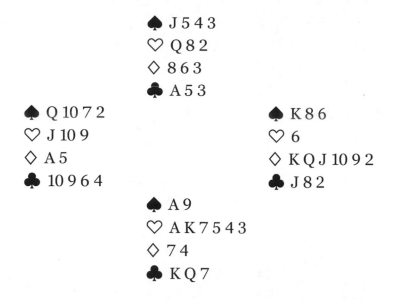

♠ J 5 4 3
♡ Q 8 2
◇ 8 6 3
♣ A 5 3

♠ Q 10 7 2
♡ J 10 9
◇ A 5
♣ 10 9 6 4

♠ K 8 6
♡ 6
◇ K Q J 10 9 2
♣ J 8 2

♠ A 9
♡ A K 7 5 4 3
◇ 7 4
♣ K Q 7

South bid 2♡ after East's Weak 2◇ Bid and bid 4♡ after North's 3♡ raise. As West led the ◇ Ace, South reassured North, "I've got a good hand, partner, with diamond shortness."

West continued with the ◇5 at Trick 2. East won with the ◇K and tried to cash the ◇J. Declarer ruffed with the ♡K. He cashed the ♡AQ, hoping for a 2-2 trump split.

Down one, losing one heart, two diamonds, and eventually one spade.

"Partner, why are you getting into a fight you can dodge but probably can't win," asked North?

What did North mean? How could South have dodged adroitly?

The chance of a 2-2 trump split were under 50%, and likely far under given East's Weak 2◇ bid.

Rather than get into a trump fight where he was an underdog on the fight card, South should discard his spade loser at Trick 3, a loser-on-loser play.

If East persists with a fourth diamond, declarer can overruff in dummy. Making 4♡, losing three diamonds but no spades.

DEAL # 38 ANOTHER DECLARE OR DEFEND

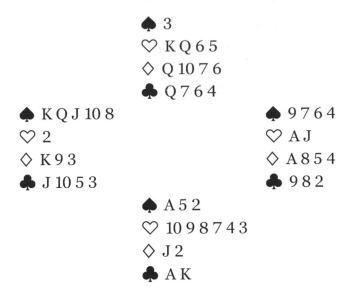

♠ 3
♡ K Q 6 5
♢ Q 10 7 6
♣ Q 7 6 4

♠ K Q J 10 8
♡ 2
♢ K 9 3
♣ J 10 5 3

♠ 9 7 6 4
♡ A J
♢ A 8 5 4
♣ 9 8 2

♠ A 5 2
♡ 10 9 8 7 4 3
♢ J 2
♣ A K

South opened 1♡, West overcalled 1♠ and everyone started raising. When the smoke cleared, South was declarer in 5♡. Yes, a diamond lead would have defeated the contract but after the ♠ King lead, do you want to declare or defend?

Declarer won the opening lead and cashed the ♣AK. He crossed to dummy with a spade ruff and discarded a diamond on the ♣Q. Declarer led the ♡K. East won and cashed the ♢A. Declarer took the rest.

Well, declarer or defend?

Defend? How? Yes, underlead the diamond ace to West's king. Another club play and you have promoted your ♡J into the setting trick. Very good!

Declare? How would you overcome that good defense? Yes, after taking a discard on the ♣Q, play a fourth club yourself discarding your last diamond.
This a loser-on-loser play will sever their communication and prevent the trump promotion.

Thanks to Frank Stewart for this most interesting deal.

DEAL # 39 DOUBLE YOUR PLEASURE

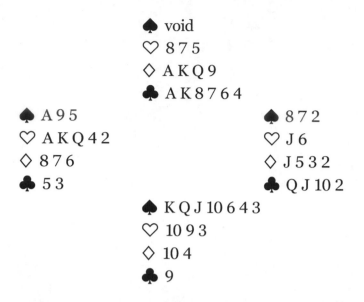

♠ void
♡ 8 7 5
♦ A K Q 9
♣ A K 8 7 6 4

♠ A 9 5   ♠ 8 7 2
♡ A K Q 4 2   ♡ J 6
♦ 8 7 6   ♦ J 5 3 2
♣ 5 3   ♣ Q J 10 2

♠ K Q J 10 6 4 3
♡ 10 9 3
♦ 10 4
♣ 9

South opened 3♠ and everyone passed. West led the ♡ Ace.

At Trick 1, East played the ♡J. Seeing the dummy, West could count three heart tricks if East had a doubleton heart and one spade trick. Where was a fifth trick?

West cashed the ♡KQ, East discarding a small diamond at Trick 3.
How should West continue the defense?

There can't be any side losers. Look at the dummy. West led the ♡4. East knew both the ♡4 and ♡2 were left so he discarded. Declarer ruffed, knocked out the spade ace and made three spades.

"My fault," said West facetiously. "Maybe if I had led the ♡2 you would have ruffed, but then you probably would have ruffed with the ♠2 anyhow."

East had a chance for an unusual double uppercut. East must ruff the fourth heart with the ♠7. Then when West wins the ♠A and leads the ♡2, East must ruff with the ♠8. Now finally West's ♠9 is the setting trick.

DEAL # 40 A GIFT? NO THANKS

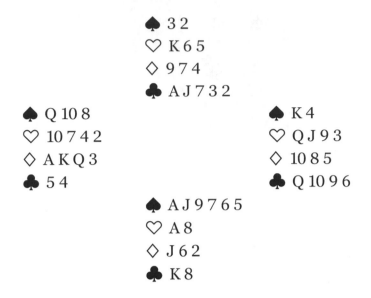

♠ 3 2
♡ K 6 5
♢ 9 7 4
♣ A J 7 3 2

♠ Q 10 8
♡ 10 7 4 2
♢ A K Q 3
♣ 5 4

♠ K 4
♡ Q J 9 3
♢ 10 8 5
♣ Q 10 9 6

♠ A J 9 7 6 5
♡ A 8
♢ J 6 2
♣ K 8

South opened 1♠ and North bid 1NT, forcing for one round. South's 2♠ rebid ended the auction. West led the ♢Ace.

West continued the ♢KQ, everyone following. How should West continue?

West switched to the ♡10. Declarer won, played the ♠A and a low spade losing two trump tricks, and took eight tricks: four spades, two hearts, and two clubs.

Could the defense have taken six before declarer took eight?

Yes had West led the thirteenth diamond at Trick 4. That gives declarer a ruff/sluff but one he cannot benefit from. If dummy ruffs, East can overruff forcing declarer to ruff. And declarer has no losers to discard from his hand.

If East is alert enough to uppercut by ruffing with the ♠K, West's trumps all become eventual winners. When East ruffs the last diamond with the spade king (please don't tell me your partner ruffed low), the defense has an extra trump trick.

Down one.

DEAL # 41 HELP PLEASE

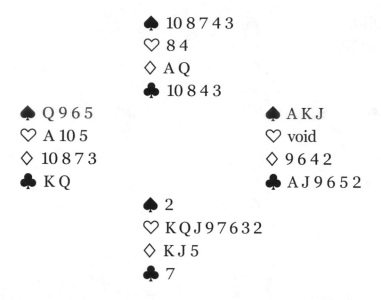

♠ 10 8 7 4 3
♡ 8 4
◇ A Q
♣ 10 8 4 3

♠ Q 9 6 5   ♠ A K J
♡ A 10 5   ♡ void
◇ 10 8 7 3   ◇ 9 6 4 2
♣ K Q   ♣ A J 9 6 5 2

♠ 2
♡ K Q J 9 7 6 3 2
◇ K J 5
♣ 7

East opened 1♣ and South bid 4♡. West's double was followed by three passes. West led the ♣ King.

West won Trick 1 with the ♣K as East encouraged. She continued with the ♣Q. East encouraged again as declarer discarded a spade.

West shifted to a diamond. Declarer won, forced out the ace of trumps and claimed the rest.

Making four hearts doubled.

Who was to blame for this result?

East needed to overtake the ♣Q at Trick 2. If declarer ruffs and leads a high trump, West can win and reach East with a spade. Another club will promote the ♡10.

If declarer discards at Trick 2, East can continue with another club. Declarer ruffs high but West discards and has two trump tricks.

DEAL # 42 TAKING ALL YOUR TRICKS

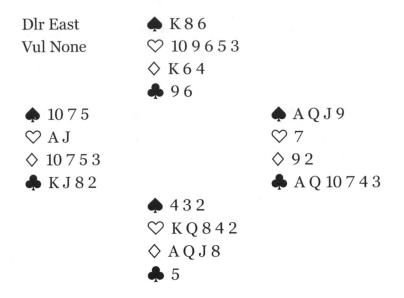

Dlr East
Vul None

♠ K 8 6
♡ 10 9 6 5 3
♢ K 6 4
♣ 9 6

♠ 10 7 5
♡ A J
♢ 10 7 5 3
♣ K J 8 2

♠ A Q J 9
♡ 7
♢ 9 2
♣ A Q 10 7 4 3

♠ 4 3 2
♡ K Q 8 4 2
♢ A Q J 8
♣ 5

East opened 1♣ and South overcalled 1♡. West raised to 2♣ and North bid 2♡. West bid 2♠. East bid 3♣ and South bid 3♢. North bid 4♡.

Should West bid 5♣ or double? West doubled, taking a likely sure plus, but East/West can make 5♣ for plus 400.

West led the ♣ 2.

East won Trick 1 with the ace. He returned the club four, declarer ruffed and led the ♡K. West won but was uncertain what to return. He led a diamond.

South escaped for down one, minus 100. A good result for North/South.

How could East/West have taken all their tricks?

East should return the club queen at Trick 2. He knows from the bidding South will ruff, but West will know to return the spade ten, not a diamond.

In addition, after three rounds of spades, the lead of the thirteenth spade gives West a trump promotion.

Down three, minus 500. Not a good result for North/South.

DEAL # 43 TRYING FOR A KNOCKOUT

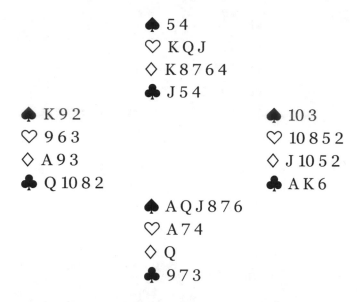

♠ 5 4
♡ K Q J
♢ K 8 7 6 4
♣ J 5 4

♠ K 9 2
♡ 9 6 3
♢ A 9 3
♣ Q 10 8 2

♠ 10 3
♡ 10 8 5 2
♢ J 10 5 2
♣ A K 6

♠ A Q J 8 7 6
♡ A 7 4
♢ Q
♣ 9 7 3

South opened 1♠ and rebid 2♠ after North bid 1NT. West led the ♣ 2.

East won the ♣AK and returned a club to West's queen as declarer followed. West, looking at the king and especially the nine of trumps, continued another club.

When East correctly ruffed high with the spade ten, West smiled to himself. When declarer discarded the diamond queen instead of overruffing, West's smile disappeared.

"Partner, what went wrong?" asked a dejected East.

What was East referring to?

Before trying for an uppercut, it's necessary to cash any quick outside winners to prevent what just happened above. Failing to do so means just trading tricks.

Declarer is not going to get into a trump fight with you and get knocked out with an uppercut.

DEAL # 44 PATIENCE PAYS OFF

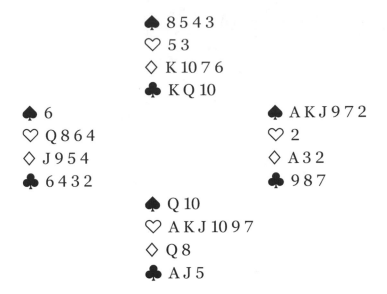

♠ 8 5 4 3
♡ 5 3
♢ K 10 7 6
♣ K Q 10

♠ 6
♡ Q 8 6 4
♢ J 9 5 4
♣ 6 4 3 2

♠ A K J 9 7 2
♡ 2
♢ A 3 2
♣ 9 8 7

♠ Q 10
♡ A K J 10 9 7
♢ Q 8
♣ A J 5

East opened 1♠ and South overcalled 2♡. After two passes, East bid 2♠. South persisted with 3♡ ending the auction. West led the ♠ 6.

West won Trick 1 with the ♠K and continued with the ♠A. When South's ♠Q fell, West led the ♠J. Declarer ruffed with the ♡9 and West overruffed with the ♡Q. West led a diamond to East who continued with the ♠9. Declarer ruffed with the ♡10, drew trumps and claimed the rest. Making three hearts.

Could you have found a more successful defense?

As usual, it's best not to overruff with trump winners, only with trump losers. If West discards at Trick 3, watch what happens.

Declarer can lead the ♡AK, then the ♡J. West wins the ♡Q and leads to East's ♢A. Now West plays the ♠9. What can South do?

His trump holding is ♡107 and West still has the ♡8, the setting trick. It's like magic, pulling an eight out of a hat.

DEAL # 45 THE FROG

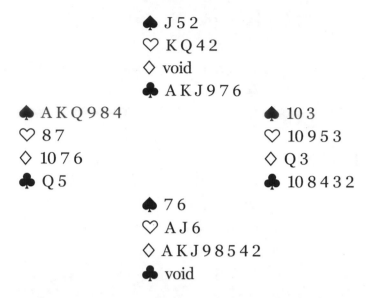

♠ J 5 2
♡ K Q 4 2
◇ void
♣ A K J 9 7 6

♠ A K Q 9 8 4   ♠ 10 3
♡ 8 7   ♡ 10 9 5 3
◇ 10 7 6   ◇ Q 3
♣ Q 5   ♣ 10 8 4 3 2

♠ 7 6
♡ A J 6
◇ A K J 9 8 5 4 2
♣ void

South opened 1◇ and West overcalled 1♠. North bid 2♣ and South rebid 3◇. When North bid 3♡, South jumped to 5◇.

West led the ♠ King.

West continued with the ♠AQ, East discarding on the third round. Declarer ruffed the third round, drew trumps and claimed.

West said, "Wyncha ruff my queen of spades with your queen of diamonds?"
East countered with "Wyncha lead your four of spades to tell me I had to?"
What was East referring to?

West knows both East and South started with two spades. The best chance for another trick is a trump promotion. If East has any honor, an uppercut will defeat the contract.

West should lead a low spade, the ♠4, at Trick 3, an Alarm Clock lead to wake up East to the need of an uppercut at Trick 3. This uppercut demand will force East to ruff (high, of course). A better play than to expect East to know to ruff West's high honor.

The ◇10 will be the setting trick. Kantar called this a case of a frog turning into a prince.

DEAL # 46 HONEST ABE

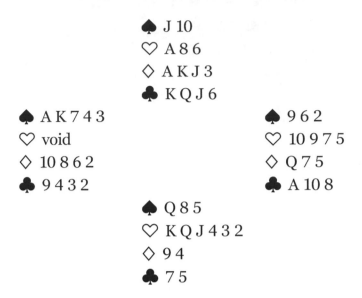

                ♠ J 10
                ♡ A 8 6
                ◇ A K J 3
                ♣ K Q J 6

♠ A K 7 4 3   ♠ 9 6 2
♡ void   ♡ 10 9 7 5
◇ 10 8 6 2   ◇ Q 7 5
♣ 9 4 3 2   ♣ A 10 8

                ♠ Q 8 5
                ♡ K Q J 4 3 2
                ◇ 9 4
                ♣ 7 5

In a team game with IMP scoring, South opened a Weak 2♡ Bid and North bid 4♡. West led the ♠ Ace.

West continued the ♠K. East played the 2, then the 6 at Tricks 1 and 2. West switched to a club. East won the ♣A. Declarer won the return and drew trumps. Making four hearts.

Her teammates had gone down one. "How could you," she asked?

It was easy. East looking at the dummy saw little hope. But at Trick 1 he played the spade nine. When West continued with the spade king, East completed his high-low with the spade two. West led a third spade.

Declarer had been watching the cards. Fearing an overruff, and with solid hearts, declarer ruffed Trick 3 with dummy's heart ace.

East had now promoted a trump trick for himself.

You can't trust anyone these days.

DEAL # 47 A RUFF/SLUFF? HELP YOURSELF

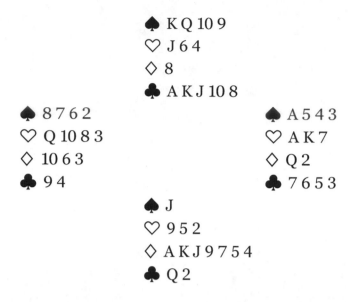

♠ K Q 10 9
♡ J 6 4
◇ 8
♣ A K J 10 8

♠ 8 7 6 2
♡ Q 10 8 3
◇ 10 6 3
♣ 9 4

♠ A 5 4 3
♡ A K 7
◇ Q 2
♣ 7 6 5 3

♠ J
♡ 9 5 2
◇ A K J 9 7 5 4
♣ Q 2

North opened 1♣, South responded 1◇, and North bid 1♠. South bid 3◇. With no fit and no extras North passed.

West led the ♡ 3.

East won Trick 1 with the ♡K and continued with the ♡A. At Trick 3 he played a third heart to West's ♡Q. West knew South was void and afraid of presenting declarer with a ruff/sluff, switched to a spade.

West won the ace, but the defense was finished. Whether declarer took a trump finesse or played for the drop, the contract was coming home.

Do you see another trick for the defense?

Ruff/sluff, who cares? What's declarer going to sluff?

If West plays the last heart at Trick 4, and East is alert to ruff with the ◇Q, West's ◇10 is the setting trick.

47

DEAL # 48 KEEP HITTING THEM

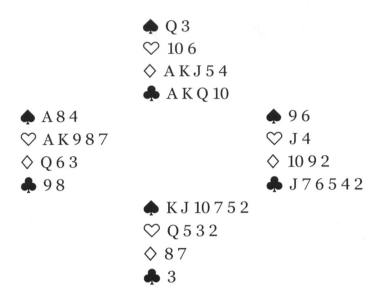

♠ Q 3
♥ 10 6
♦ A K J 5 4
♣ A K Q 10

♠ A 8 4
♥ A K 9 8 7
♦ Q 6 3
♣ 9 8

♠ 9 6
♥ J 4
♦ 10 9 2
♣ J 7 6 5 4 2

♠ K J 10 7 5 2
♥ Q 5 3 2
♦ 8 7
♣ 3

West opened 1♥ and North overcalled 2♦. East passed and South bid 2♠. North bid 3♣ and when South bid 3♠, North bid 4♠. West led the ♥ Ace.

West continued with the ♥K and led a third heart. Declarer ruffed with dummy's queen to avoid being overruffed. He cashed the ♣AK, discarding his last heart and led a spade to his king. West won the ace and led a diamond. Declarer finished the trumps.

Making four spades, losing two hearts and one spade.

Do you see a line of play to defeat four spades?

Again, West should just keep on hitting declarer with those hearts. And East must be alert to ruff the fourth round of hearts with the ♠9.
When declarer overruffs with the ♠10, West has the ♠84 behind declarer's ♠J5.

The ♠8 is the setting trick. A little persistence but worth the wait.
Down one.

DEAL # 49 DIFFICULT, BUT COUNT THE TRICKS

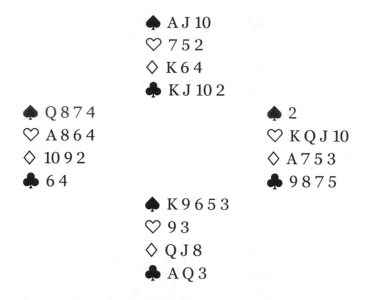

♠ A J 10
♥ 7 5 2
♦ K 6 4
♣ K J 10 2

♠ Q 8 7 4
♥ A 8 6 4
♦ 10 9 2
♣ 6 4

♠ 2
♥ K Q J 10
♦ A 7 5 3
♣ 9 8 7 5

♠ K 9 6 5 3
♥ 9 3
♦ Q J 8
♣ A Q 3

This was a difficult deal Mike Lawrence showed on his excellent website BridgeClues a few years ago. After North opened 1♣, East overcalled his strong four-card heart suit. South responded 1♠ and eventually wound up in 4♠. West led the ♥ Ace.

At Trick 2, West continued the ♥4 to East. South ruffed the third heart and led the ♠3 to dummy's ♠10. Declarer then led the ♦4 from dummy, East played low, and South won the queen.

Declarer took another spade finesse, then cashed the spade ace. He came to his hand with the ♣2 and cashed the spade king, drawing the last trump.
Ten tricks: Four spades, one heart ruff, four clubs, and one diamond.

How could the defense have played to defeat the contract?

East can count the same tricks. If West has four spades to the king, declarer is always down. To cater to the above lie, East must win the first diamond and make the unusual play of another heart, offering a useless ruff/sluff.

What can declarer do? If he ruffs in dummy, he can't repeat the trump finesse. If he ruffs in hand, West has more trumps than declarer and will score a trump trick.

DEAL # 50 DON'T GET TRUMP ENDPLAYED

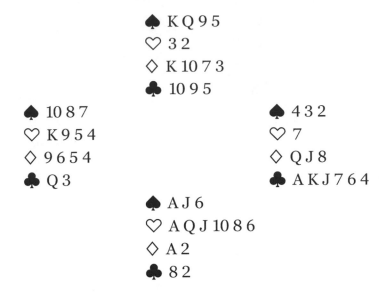

♠ K Q 9 5
♥ 3 2
♦ K 10 7 3
♣ 10 9 5

♠ 10 8 7
♥ K 9 5 4
♦ 9 6 5 4
♣ Q 3

♠ 4 3 2
♥ 7
♦ Q J 8
♣ A K J 7 6 4

♠ A J 6
♥ A Q J 10 8 6
♦ A 2
♣ 8 2

South opened 1♥, North bid 1♠ and East overcalled 2♣. When South bid 3♥, North raised to 4♥. West led the ♣ Queen.

East won the first two club tricks and continued with the club jack. Declarer ruffed with the heart queen. West knew she should try to promote her heart nine by not overruffing. She discarded a diamond.

Declarer played the ♦AK and ruffed a diamond. He then cashed three rounds of spades. With four cards to be played, West held ♥ K 9 5 4 while declarer held the ♥ A J 10 8. South played the ♥ J.

Whether West won this trick or the next, she was trump endplayed and could only score one trump trick.

How would you have defended as West? Was not overruffing correct?

West was correct not overruffing. But instead of discarding a diamond, West had to discard a spade to avoid this endplay. Then she could have ruffed the third spade and exited a heart.

Thanks again to Mike Lawrence for another most interesting deal.

DEAL # 51 DON'T UPPERCUT YOURSELF

One of the biggest mistakes inexperienced declarers make is a failure of hand type recognition. There are only a certain number of hand types. If you properly recognize what type you are facing, you probably know how to proceed.

One of the most common misplays I see is the urge to ruff in the dummy.

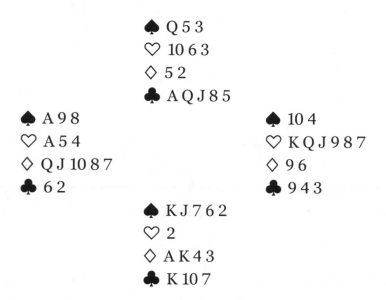

East opened a Weak 2♡ Bid, South overcalled 2♠, West and North raised and South reached 4♠. West led the ◇ Queen.

Without hesitation, declarer won the ◇A at Trick 1, cashed the ◇K and ruffed a diamond. The ruff-in-the-dummy ASAP syndrome. East overruffed and led the ♡K. West overtook with the ace to play another diamond.

Declarer had to ruff this trick with the ♠Q. Now West had the ♠A98 over declarer's ♠KJ762, good for two more tricks.

A simple second suit hand - clubs. Draw the trumps, lose two aces, eleven easy tricks. Hand recognition.

51

DEAL # 52 ONLY ONE PLACE LEFT

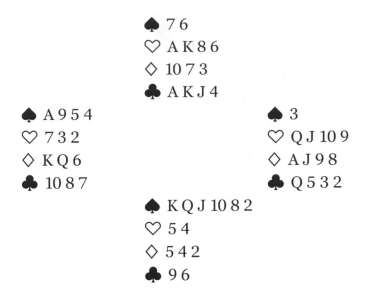

                ♠ 7 6
                ♡ A K 8 6
                ♢ 10 7 3
                ♣ A K J 4

♠ A 9 5 4   ♠ 3
♡ 7 3 2   ♡ Q J 10 9
♢ K Q 6   ♢ A J 9 8
♣ 10 8 7   ♣ Q 5 3 2

                ♠ K Q J 10 8 2
                ♡ 5 4
                ♢ 5 4 2
                ♣ 9 6

South opened a Weak 2♠ Bid. North bid 2NT, asking for a feature, an outside ace or king. South rebid 3♠, denying a feature and North passed.

West led the ♢ King.

West won Trick 1 and continued with the ♢Q. He led a third diamond to East's ♢A, South following each time. East switched to the ♡Q. Declarer won, knocked out the ace of trumps, drew the rest of the trumps, and claimed.

Could the defenders have done better? Where were more tricks possible?

East should assume South has a six-card spade suit, likely with no feature. He has already shown three diamonds so how many other cards are left?

Four outside of spades. And in the dummy, even the caddy can see the ♡AK and the ♣AK. So there are no tricks coming in hearts or clubs.

If the defense is going to win two more tricks, they can only come from the trump suit. East must play his last diamond. Declarer will ruff high and if West discards, (let's hope so), West will take two trump tricks in time.

Down one.

DEAL # 53 A TRUMP PROMOTION ADDICT

Trump promotion is not always right even when it looks so obvious.
Here is a deal from the Bridge Bulletin Sept 2019, by Mike Lawrence.

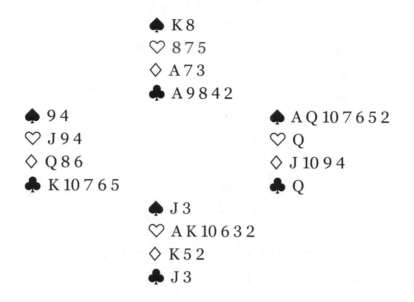

```
                    ♠ K 8
                    ♡ 8 7 5
                    ◇ A 7 3
                    ♣ A 9 8 4 2
    ♠ 9 4                           ♠ A Q 10 7 6 5 2
    ♡ J 9 4                         ♡ Q
    ◇ Q 8 6                         ◇ J 10 9 4
    ♣ K 10 7 6 5                    ♣ Q
                    ♠ J 3
                    ♡ A K 10 6 3 2
                    ◇ K 5 2
                    ♣ J 3
```

South opened 1♡ and North bid 2♣. East bid 3♠. After South and West passed, North carried on to 4♡. West led the ♠ 9.

East took the first two spade tricks and considered how to continue. Meanwhile South was thinking, "I've lost two tricks already, I have a club and diamond loser, and hearts are probably not 2/2. I'm going down at least two."

Without the benefit of seeing all four hands, consider East's problem. A safe heart or diamond exit? The singleton club? He decided to try for a trump promotion and played a spade. Maybe West had three hearts to the ten?

South discarded a club, West ruffed with the heart nine, and declarer discarded a diamond from dummy. A double discard play, a sluff/sluff.

Being able now to ruff a diamond in dummy and no club loser, the defense heard those dreaded words, "I claim."

Ten tricks. Sometimes too much knowledge can be dangerous.

DEAL # 54 SPEEDING TICKET

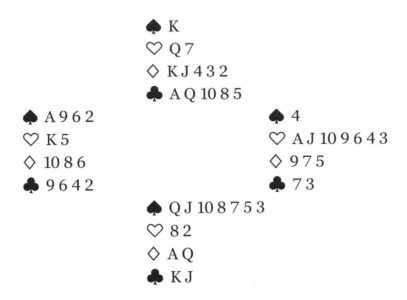

♠ K
♡ Q 7
◇ K J 4 3 2
♣ A Q 10 8 5

♠ A 9 6 2   ♠ 4
♡ K 5   ♡ A J 10 9 6 4 3
◇ 10 8 6   ◇ 9 7 5
♣ 9 6 4 2   ♣ 7 3

♠ Q J 10 8 7 5 3
♡ 8 2
◇ A Q
♣ K J

South opened 1♠ and North bid 2◇, game forcing. East bid 3♡.
South continued with 4♠, ending the auction. West led the ♡ King.

The ♡K won Trick 1 as East signaled with the ♡10. How should West continue?

West made the 'natural' play of another heart. East won the ♡A and played a third heart. Declarer ruffed in dummy and West was limited to one spade trick, now or later. Making four spades.

How could the defense have prevailed?

West played too fast at Trick 2. He should cash the ♠A before continuing a second heart. Now the third heart lead from East will promote West's ♠9 to the setting trick.

Speed kills.

DEAL # 55 LOSE TO AVOID AN UPPERCUT

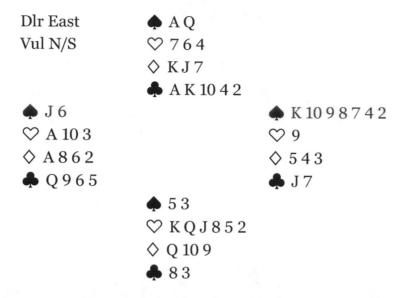

Dlr East
Vul N/S

♠ A Q
♡ 7 6 4
♢ K J 7
♣ A K 10 4 2

♠ J 6
♡ A 10 3
♢ A 8 6 2
♣ Q 9 6 5

♠ K 10 9 8 7 4 2
♡ 9
♢ 5 4 3
♣ J 7

♠ 5 3
♡ K Q J 8 5 2
♢ Q 10 9
♣ 8 3

East opened 3♠. When South and West passed, North bid 3NT. South was not playing any conventions and bid 4♡. (Many play after a 3NT overcall that 4♣ asks about hand strength, 4♢ and 4♡ are transfers). West led the ♠ Jack.

Declarer, anxious to draw trumps won the ♠A at Trick 1 and led a heart to the ♡K. West won the ♡A and led the ♠6. East won the ♠K and returned a third spade.

Declarer could not prevent West from scoring his ♡10 for the setting trick. Down one.

Could you have avoided the uppercut?

It depends on how many spades you think East has. If he has eight spades and no entry, the above line will be successful. But if East has seven spades, more likely, declarer should take the finesse at Trick 1, 'knowing' it will lose.

But a spade return at Trick 2 doesn't hurt. When West wins the heart ace, West has no spades and East has no entry. The contract is safe.

DEAL # 56 COUNT YOUR TRICKS

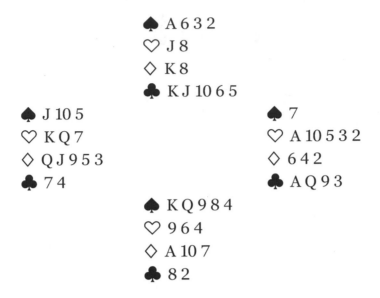

        ♠ A 6 3 2
        ♡ J 8
        ♢ K 8
        ♣ K J 10 6 5

♠ J 10 5   ♠ 7
♡ K Q 7   ♡ A 10 5 3 2
♢ Q J 9 5 3   ♢ 6 4 2
♣ 7 4   ♣ A Q 9 3

        ♠ K Q 9 8 4
        ♡ 9 6 4
        ♢ A 10 7
        ♣ 8 2

North opened 1♣, East overcalled 1♡, and South bid 1♠. Everyone started raising and when the smoke cleared, South was declaring 3♠.

West led the ♡ King.

How should East defend? He could count two heart tricks and one or two club tricks depending on how many clubs declarer had. He played the heart deuce at Trick 1, but this was an attitude card. West switched to the ♢Q.

Declarer lost four tricks: two clubs and two hearts, making three spades.

Could you have found another trick?

When there are no more winners, think what? Trump promotion. If West and South each have two clubs, a third round may promote a trump trick for West. But how can East get West to switch to a club? The ♡2 was attitude.

Take over! Overtake the ♡K with the ace and return the ♡2. Now that shouts for a club. After winning the ♡Q, a club shift and three rounds of clubs promotes a trump trick for West.

Down one, losing two hearts, two clubs, and one spade.

DEAL # 57 JUST ENOUGH

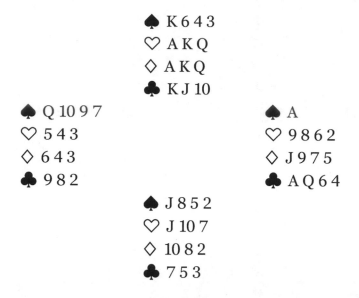

```
              ♠ K 6 4 3
              ♡ A K Q
              ◇ A K Q
              ♣ K J 10
♠ Q 10 9 7                      ♠ A
♡ 5 4 3                         ♡ 9 8 6 2
◇ 6 4 3                         ◇ J 9 7 5
♣ 9 8 2                         ♣ A Q 6 4
              ♠ J 8 5 2
              ♡ J 10 7
              ◇ 10 8 2
              ♣ 7 5 3
```

Playing in a Board-A-Match (BAM) where every trick mattered, North opened 2♣, strong and artificial. South responded 2◇, North bid 2♡, conventionally forcing South to bid 2♠. Then North bid 2NT, game forcing,

24+ HCP, a hand too good to bid a non-forcing 2NT after 2◇.

South, though 4333, bid 3♣, Stayman and ended in 4♠, but with South as declarer. West led the ♣ 2.

East won the first two club tricks and exited a third club. Declarer led a trump. East won the ace and returned a passive diamond. Declarer, sure that trumps were 4-1, cashed two more rounds of diamonds, then three rounds of hearts.

He then played a low trump from both hands. West won and was endplayed. He had to lead away from his remaining ♠ Q10. Declarer was down one.

Sitting E/W, how do you think your team did on this board? A push?

The other North ended in 3NT, down one, to push the board.

If the first East had continued a fourth club after winning the spade ace, West would have scored two trump tricks, beating 4♠ two tricks winning the board.

DEAL # 58 KEEP'EM COMING

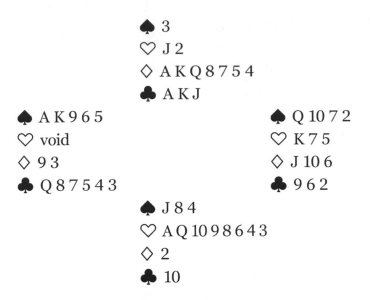

♠ 3
♡ J 2
◇ A K Q 8 7 5 4
♣ A K J

♠ A K 9 6 5   ♠ Q 10 7 2
♡ void   ♡ K 7 5
◇ 9 3   ◇ J 10 6
♣ Q 8 7 5 4 3   ♣ 9 6 2

♠ J 8 4
♡ A Q 10 9 8 6 4 3
◇ 2
♣ 10

South opened 4♡. North bid Blackwood, then 6♡. West led the ♠ King

At Trick 1, East followed with the ♠10. What did that mean? What should that mean? I have the queen? Suit preference for diamonds? Continue the spade suit? Count?

You can see all four hands, but West was in a quandary. He shifted to a diamond.

Declarer picked up the trump suit with two finesses and made the slam.

What should West be thinking at Trick 2?

A diamond shift seems illogical. More likely, a continuation is best. East is encouraging the best he can.

If West plays another spade forcing dummy to ruff, declarer cannot pick up East's trump king.

Declarer can only finesse once in hearts. Down one.

DEAL # 59 EXPERT THINKING

From the Fall 2020 Online Knockout reported in the Bridge World, April 2022.

				North	
Dlr East				♠ 10 9 4	
Vul E/W				♡ J 3 2	
East	South	West	North	◇ J 7 5	
Bramley	Rodwell	Woolsey	Meckstroth	♣ A 9 5 2	East
1♣*	1◇	Dbl^	2◇		♠ A K 8 7 6
2♠	3◇	All Pass			♡ A 6
					◇ 8 2
• 16+ HCP		^ 5-8 HCP			♣ K J 10 4

Opening   Lead: ♠ Queen

Woolsey led the ♠Q and continued a spade. Bramley won the ♠K at Trick 2, then the ♠A, suggesting suit preference for clubs. Woolsey discarded a discouraging ♡10, upside-down attitude. How should East continue to Trick 4?

East knew if West had nothing in hearts, he must have the ♣Q. He shifted to the ♣J. Rodwell, the declarer, won, cashed the ◇AK and had nine tricks: six diamonds, one club, and two hearts.

Were there any clues to finding a successful defense?

Woolsey wrote that East "was afraid declarer might have KQ doubleton of hearts and two low clubs...several clues pointing towards continuing spades:

I very likely had the ◇Q to have 5 HCP.

The most important clue....if I didn't...Bart wouldn't be on lead at this point, because I would have ruffed his ♠A and led a club to prevent him from continuing spades.

As I hadn't....I must have a diamond honor...continuing spades will...defeat the contract." The uppercut with the ◇Q is the setting trick.

West: ♠ Q 3
         ♡ 10 9 8 7 5   ♠ J 5 2 South
         ◇ Q 3   ♡ K Q 4
         ♣ Q 8 6 3   ◇ A K 10 9 6 4
                  ♣ 7

DEAL # 60 ANOTHER DEAL FROM THE SAME EVENT

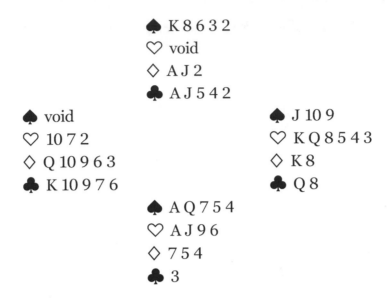

♠ K 8 6 3 2
♡ void
◇ A J 2
♣ A J 5 4 2

♠ void
♡ 10 7 2
◇ Q 10 9 6 3
♣ K 10 9 7 6

♠ J 10 9
♡ K Q 8 5 4 3
◇ K 8
♣ Q 8

♠ A Q 7 5 4
♡ A J 9 6
◇ 7 5 4
♣ 3

Both teams reached 6♠ and the opening lead at each table was the ♡2.

How would you play this slam? At one table, declarer drew one round of trumps and then embarked on a cross-ruff. Club to the ace, club ruff, heart ruff, club ruff as East discarded a heart.

Then another heart ruff and a club ruff. But this time East ruffed, overruffed by declarer. Now East could not be prevented from scoring a trump trick.

What was the successful line of play?

Expert Bart Bramley, after winning the heart ace at Trick I, started the cross-ruff immediately, leaving the trump suit alone. Club to the ace, club ruff, heart ruff, club ruffed and overruffed, heart ruff, another club ruffed and overruffed.

Then a high spade: twelve tricks.

It would not have helped East to discard a diamond on one of the clubs. South would cash the ace of diamonds and continue the cross-ruff.

Well done, Bart.

PART II

Quiz   Deals

The following deals show only your hand and the dummy. Try to decide how to continue the defense before looking at the entire deal below.

DEAL # 61 JUST MAYBE

North
♠ J 10 4
♡ A Q 8 3
◇ 6
♣ K Q J 6 2

East
♠ Q 8 7 2
♡ 9 7 6 5
◇ 9 7 5 2
♣ 5

North	East	South	West
1♣	P	1♡	2◇
2♡^	4◇	4♡	All Pass

^ Four trump

Opening Lead: ♠ Ace

West led the ♠A, East played an encouraging eight. West continued with the ♠K and a spade to East's queen, declarer following each time.

How should East continue the defense?

West would have cashed an ace if he had one. East hopefully played a club, not wanting to give declarer a ruff/sluff. Declarer won, drew trumps, and claimed.

Was there a more successful line of defense?

Since East was correct – West does not have any minor aces, the only possible trick is a trump trick. If West has a singleton ♡J or ♡10, a fourth spade might promote a trump trick. Declarer has nothing to sluff.

Another spade lets West ruff with the heart ten, forcing dummy's queen, promoting a trump trick for East.

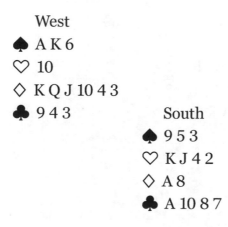

West
♠ A K 6
♡ 10
◇ K Q J 10 4 3
♣ 9 4 3

South
♠ 9 5 3
♡ K J 4 2
◇ A 8
♣ A 10 8 7

DEAL # 62 BOLD PLAY

North
♠ Q J
♡ Q 9 8
♢ Q J 10 3
♣ Q 7 5 4

South	West	North	East
1♠	P	1NT*	P
2♡	P	2NT	P
3♡	P	4♡	All Pass

West
♠ 8 6
♡ J 10 6
♢ K 8 2
♣ A K 10 8 3

* Forcing, one round

Opening Lead: ♣ Ace

Danny Kleinman always says that hands with three queens should strive to play in notrump. He said with four queens, a "Sultan's Harem," to strive even harder. But when South showed 5/5 in the majors, North bid 4♡.

West started with the ♣AK, East played the ♣9, then the ♣6 as declarer followed twice. Thinking trump promotion, West continued with the ♣3. East with the ♡74, ruffed high, waiting for the applause.

Do you think the kibitzers were applauding or was declarer claiming?

West should know after Trick 2 declarer's shape is most likely 5=5=1=2. If the declarer has the ♢A, nothing matters. But he should have remembered the need to cash side winners next. Declarer discarded his diamond loser at Trick 3.

West needed to make a very good play of first cashing or trying to cash the ♢K at Trick 3, then try for the trump promotion. Now the kibitzers would be cheering.

East:
♠ 9 7 4 2
♡ 7 4
♢ A 9 7 5 4
♣ 9 6

South
♠ A K 10 5 3
♡ A K 5 3 2
♢ 6
♣ J 2

DEAL # 63 WHICH?

North
♠ 9 8 7
♡ Q 8 6 4 3
♦ K Q J
♣ A 5

East
♠ K 4
♡ 10 7
♦ A 3 2
♣ Q J 10 9 8 7

North	East	South	West
1♡	2♣	2♠	P
3♠	P	4♠	All Pass

Opening   Lead: ♡   Ace

West led the ♡AK, declarer followed with the 5 and jack as East echoed to show two. West continued with the ♡2, dummy played the six and East ruffed with the ♠4. Declarer overruffed with the ♠5 and played three rounds of trump starting with the ace.

He lost a trick to the diamond ace, making four spades.

Did you do any better as East?

East, after seeing partner's ♡AK should know declarer likely has all the missing high cards. His ♠K is going nowhere. Even if by some miracle partner has the ♠ A or Q, the contract will be set. No matter what, it cannot hurt to ruff Trick 3 with the ♠K. Now partner's ♠10 is the setting trick.

As Danny says, "Never send a toddler to do a man's job."

West
♠ 10 3 2
♡ A K 9 2
♦ 9 7 4
♣ 4 3 2

South
♠ A Q J 6 5
♡ J 5
♦ 10 8 6 5
♣ K 6

DEAL # 64 IT'S YOUR DAY

East	South	West	North
P	1♡	2♠^	3◇
P	3♡	P	3♠
Dbl*	4♡	All	Pass

*Spade honor

^ Weak jump overcall

Opening Lead: ♠ Ace

North
♠ 7 5 4
♡ 3
◇ A K J 10 9 8
♣ K 9 3

East
♠ Q 9
♡ J 5
◇ 7 4 3 2
♣ Q 8 5 4 2

West led the ♠AK and continued with the ♠J. East discarded and declarer ruffed. Declarer cashed the ♡AK, West followed with the ♡96. Making four hearts, losing two spades and one heart.

Could the defense have done anything differently?

West could have led a low spade, knowing East had the queen but that didn't matter. With no other outside tricks, the defense needs two trump tricks. If East ruffs the spade jack with the heart jack, West's heart holding of Q96 is promoted to two tricks.

West might have helped by leading a small spade at Trick 3, forcing East to ruff, hopefully with the jack, not the five.

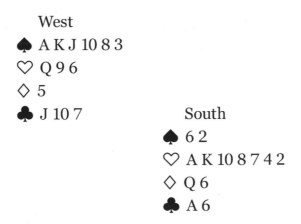

West
♠ A K J 10 8 3
♡ Q 9 6
◇ 5
♣ J 10 7

South
♠ 6 2
♡ A K 10 8 7 4 2
◇ Q 6
♣ A 6

Remember earlier, I said if you keep ruffing high, one day the kibitzers will be applauding. Today is the day.

DEAL # 65 HOPING FOR THE BEST

                            North
                            ♠ A 3 2
                            ♡ 6 5
North   South   ◇ J 3 2
1♣   1♡   ♣ A K J 7 5   East
1NT   4♡   ♠ J 10 9
All Pass   ♡ K 10 8
                                                     ◇ A 9 7 6
Opening   Lead: ◇ King   ♣ 10 9 6

West led the ◇K, East encouraged with the nine. West continued with the ◇Q and a third diamond, East winning as declarer followed to the first three tricks. How should East continue the defense?

East switched to the ♠J; Q, K, A. Declarer took two heart finesses, losing no trump tricks, then discarded her spade loser on the clubs. Making four hearts.

Would you have found a different line of defense?

If your partner has a trump honor, declarer is always going down. Otherwise, you can see the above handwriting on the wall. A better chance is if West has a higher trump than the dummy. Even the ♡7 may suffice as declarer might ruff with the ♡J from AQJ9432 and then finesse the queen.

If so, the thirteenth diamond will force declarer to ruff high. Now you have a trump trick.

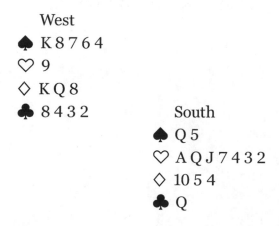

                    West
                 ♠ K 8 7 6 4
                 ♡ 9
                 ◇ K Q 8
                 ♣ 8 4 3 2   South
                                  ♠ Q 5
                                  ♡ A Q J 7 4 3 2
                                  ◇ 10 5 4
                                  ♣ Q

DEAL # 66 USE A LITTLE IMAGINATION

North
♠ K 5
♡ void
♦ A Q 10 7 5 2
♣ K Q J 9 5

East
♠ A Q 9 8 4 3
♡ 7 6
♦ J 3
♣ 8 6 4

West	North	East	South
4♡	4NT	P	5♦
	All Pass		

Opening Lead: ♠ 2

West led the ♠2 and East won the first two tricks, West showing out on the second spade. Pretty good dummy. How should East continue?

East returned a club, hoping partner had the ♣A. Sorry, Charlie. Wishful thinking. Declarer claimed.

How would you have defended?

Remember the song "When You Wish Upon A Star?" If you are going to wish, wish for something useful. If partner has the ♣A, he is always going to win it.

What other card could you wish for? C'mon, think about it.

West's hand: ♠2 ♡A Q J 10 8 4 3 2 ♦K ♣7 3 2

Now do you get it? Didn't think your ♦J was going to be the setting trick, did you? When you return a spade, West ruffs with the ♦K, dummy overruffs with the ace and voila.

DEAL # 67 ONLY HOPE

South	West	North	East		North
1♠	P	2♣	P		♠ 6 4 3
2♦	P	2♠	P		♡ A K 8
3♠	P	4♠	All Pass		♦ A 6 5
					♣ K 9 7 3

Opening Lead: ♣ 2

East
♠ K 9
♡ Q 9 7 3 2
♦ 7 3 2
♣ A Q 4

East won the club queen and cashed the club ace. He shifted to a trump. West won the queen and played a third club. Declarer won in dummy and led another trump. When East's king appeared, declarer claimed. Making four spades.

Just routine or was there a successful line of defense?

As usual, when there are no high card tricks to cash, look where? Yes, the trump suit. You never know what you might find.

East should play a third club, not a trump at Trick 3. When West wins the spade queen, she can play yet another club. West can ruff with the trump king. When declarer overruffs, West's spade eight is the setting trick.

Seek and ye shall find.

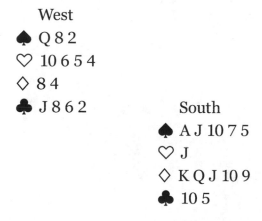

West
♠ Q 8 2
♡ 10 6 5 4
♦ 8 4
♣ J 8 6 2

South
♠ A J 10 7 5
♡ J
♦ K Q J 10 9
♣ 10 5

DEAL # 68 A FLAIR FOR THE DRAMATIC

North
♠ J 8 5 2
♡ Q J 5
◇ K 9 4
♣ 10 5 3

West
♠ Q 4
♡ 6 4 3
◇ A Q J 10 7 5
♣ Q 6

South	West	North	East
1♠	2◇	2♠	4♣*
4♡	P	4♠	All Pass

* Fit showing jump by agreement

Opening Lead: ♣ Queen

West led the ♣Q and continued with a low club. East won Trick 2 with the ♣K and continued with the ♣A, declarer following each time.

How should West defend? What should he play at Trick 3?

West, a great showman and with a flair for the dramatic, saw the perfect defense. Hoping to make the newspaper, he ruffed his partner's ♣A at Trick 3 and led the ◇A to cash the setting trick.

Whoops, declarer ruffed, drew the remaining trumps and claimed.

Do you see a line of defense to beat four spades and make the newspaper?

If declarer has a diamond, it's not going away. But if East plays the thirteenth club, West will score the ♠Q on a trump promotion.

With even greater flair, discard the ◇A at Trick 3. This in the face of North's ◇K will force East to draw the correct conclusion. With the club continuation, West will score the trump queen en passant.

As Bernie Chazen would have said, "Now that's flair, mister!"

East
♠ 10 3
♡ 10 8
◇ 8 6 3 2
♣ A K 8 4 2

South
♠ A K 9 7 6
♡ A K 9 7 2
◇ void
♣ J 9 7

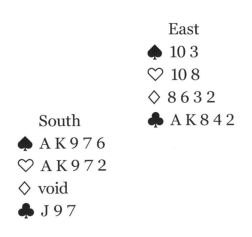

DEAL # 69 HIGH OR LOW?

North
- ♠ Q J 10 4
- ♡ 8 2
- ◇ K 3 2
- ♣ A K 5 4

West	North	East	South
1♠	P	P	3♡
P	3NT	P	4♡
All Pass			

West
- ♠ A K 8 7 5
- ♡ A 9 6 5
- ◇ Q J 10
- ♣ 6

Opening Lead: ♠ Ace

West led the ♠A; 4, 3, 9. Seeing the low discouraging spade three from East, how should West continue?

West switched to the ◇Q. Declarer won the ace and led a club to dummy. He discarded a spade on the ◇K. After knocking out the ♠K, he claimed, making four hearts with an overtrick.

"Did you think I played the spade three from ♠632," asked East?

Everything is only what it is in the mind of the beholder. After Trick 1, the only missing spade spots were the 6 and 2. East could not have started with 63 or 632. He either started with singleton 3 or 32. So West should cash a second high spade. Looking at three defensive tricks, where is the fourth?

Perhaps the heart nine? Play a third spade. East will be ruffing and perhaps the defense can create a second trump trick.

East plays the ♡7. Just high enough. When South overruffs, West has two trump tricks.

East
- ♠ 3 2
- ♡ 7
- ◇ 9 8 7 6 5 4
- ♣ 9 7 3 2

South
- ♠ 9 6
- ♡ K Q J 10 4 3
- ◇ A
- ♣ Q J 10 8

DEAL # 70 DELICATE DISCARDING

                              North
                              ♠ 10 8 6 2
                              ♡ J 6 2
                              ◇ J 7 3
            West   ♣ A Q J
            ♠ Q 4
            ♡ 10 7
            ◇ K 9 6 5 2
            ♣ 8 6 4 2

South opens 1♠ and after a 1 – 2 – 4 auction reaches 4♠.
West guesses to lead the ♡ 10.

East cashed the ♡AKQ, declarer following. West had to discard on the third heart.
He threw the diamond nine. At Trick 4 East obeyed and shifted to a diamond. Declarer
won the ace and drew trumps.

He discarded his diamond loser on dummy's long club. Making four spades.

What would you have discarded?

If partner has the club king, he is probably always getting it. But holding the ♠Q4
of trumps you know that another round of hearts will give you a trump promotion.
Forget diamonds, take the sure triumph ahead of the iffy.

Discard the two of diamonds. If East still persists with a diamond, tell him to check
your convention card.

Ask him when did you switch to upside down carding?

                              East:
                              ♠ 5
                              ♡ A K Q 8 3
                              ◇ 10 8 4
            South   ♣ 10 9 5 3
            ♠ A K J 9 7 3
            ♡ 9 5 4
            ◇ A Q
            ♣ K 7

DEAL # 71 YES OR NO? OPTIONS

North
- ♠ 8 5
- ♡ 10 6 3
- ◇ A K J 7
- ♣ Q J 7 5

East
- ♠ A K Q J 6 4
- ♡ 5 2
- ◇ 9 3
- ♣ A 8 3

South opened 1♡ and North bid 1NT, forcing for one round, planning to show a limit raise with three trumps. East bid 2♠. When South passed, North bid 3♡. South stretched a bit and bid 4♡. West led the ♠ 9.

East won the first two tricks, West following with the spade three. If West has the ♡ Jxx or ♡ Qx, another spade would promote a trump trick for the defense. East continued with the ♠Q.

Declarer ruffed high, drew the trumps, and discarded two club losers on dummy's diamonds. Making four hearts, losing two spades and one club.

How should East know what to play at Trick 3?

A trump promotion might be right or not. You can try to ask West. Play the club ace and West should tell you what to do. On the club ace, West plays the nine. Encouraging in clubs.

Do you think West wants a trump promotion or a club?

West:
- ♠ 9 3
- ♡ 9 8 4
- ◇ 10 8 6 4 2
- ♣ K 9 2

South
- ♠ 10 7 2
- ♡ A K Q J 7
- ◇ Q 5
- ♣ 10 6 4

DEAL # 72 BOTH WRONG

North
- ♠ 10 7 5 3
- ♡ A K Q 4
- ◇ K 10 5 3
- ♣ J

South opened 1♣ and North bid 1◇.
South bid 1♡ and North bid 4♡.

West
- ♠ K 9 8 4 2
- ♡ 5 3
- ◇ A J 4
- ♣ 8 7 6

West led the ♠ 4

East won the ace and returned the jack. Declarer played the queen, West the king.

How should West continue the defense from here?

West played the two of spades from his remaining ♠982. East ruffed with the heart six, declarer overruffed, drew trumps and made an overtrick.

Who would you blame for this defense?

The yelling started. West said "Ruff the third spade with your heart jack, partner. You know declarer is void too."

East thought, then yelled back "Cash your diamond ace first, otherwise, declarer will just discard his loser."

Usually he who yells first is wrong. Here both East and West contributed to the poor defense.

East:
- ♠ A J
- ♡ J 8 6
- ◇ 9 8 7 6 2
- ♣ 10 4 3

South
- ♠ Q 6
- ♡ 10 9 7 2
- ◇ Q
- ♣ A K Q 9 5 2

DEAL # 73 SIMPLE ARITHMETIC

North
♠ A 6 2
♡ K Q 7 6
♢ J 5 2
♣ K 5 3

South	North
1NT(15-17)	2♣
2♡	4♡
All Pass	

West
♠ K Q J 9 4
♡ A 5
♢ 8 6 3
♣ J 10 9

Opening Lead: ♠ King

Declarer won the opening lead with dummy's ace, East played the eight. Declarer played a diamond to his king and led a heart. How should West defend?

West won the ♡A, cashed the ♠Q as East followed with the seven. West cashed the ♠J, his third trick, and switched to the ♣J.

Declarer drew the rest of the trumps and claimed.

"Simple addition," said East. What did she mean?

West has eleven HCP, dummy has thirteen, and declarer has at least fifteen. That adds up so, let's see, using a fancy computer, 39!

Where can another trick come from if not in the trump suit? If West plays another spade, what is declarer going to sluff? If East has the ♡J, the one missing point, her ♡J8 has been promoted to the setting trick.

East
♠ 8 7
♡ J 8 4
♢ 10 9 7 4
♣ 7 6 4 2

South
♠ 10 5 3
♡ 10 9 3 2
♢ A K Q
♣ A Q 8

DEAL # 74 MAKE PARTNER DO THE RIGHT THING

	North	South	West	North	East
	♠ J 10 9 8 6				
	♡ A 6 5 3	1♡	2◇	3◇	P
	◇ K 7	3♡	P	4♡	All Pass
West	♣ K J				

West
♠ A K Q 5
♡ J 10 8
◇ A Q 8 5 4
♣ 3

West led the ♠ King. Trick 1: A; 6, 7, 3. West continued with the ♠A showing the ♠Q and East followed with the deuce. Now what? Another spade? Which one? A diamond?

West knew to cash the ◇A (good play) before trying for a trump promotion. Then she led the ♠Q (maybe not so good). East discarded (for sure not good) as declarer ruffed. Declarer drew trumps and claimed.

Who should we blame, East or West?

East might have pictured West with ♠AKQ only. But it couldn't hurt to throw the ♡9 on the table. Of course, after cashing the ◇A, West should have led the ♠5 (very good) to be sure East ruffed.

East
♠ 7 2
♡ 9
◇ 10 9 6 3 2
♣ 9 6 5 4 2

South
♠ 4 3
♡ K Q 7 4 2
◇ J
♣ A Q 10 8 7

DEAL # 75 NOT ASKING FOR MUCH

				North	
East	South	West	North	♠ A 5 4 3	
1♣	1♠	3♡^	4♠	♡ 8 5	
	All Pass			◇ K J 10 8 7	East
	^ Weak jump shift			♣ K 3	♠ Q J

Opening Lead: ♣ 9

East Hand:
♠ Q J
♡ A 10 6 2
◇ 9 3
♣ A Q 8 4 2

East won the first two club tricks and could count three winners. Where was a fourth trick? What card(s) did she need? How should the defense continue?

East tried the ♡A (good play), then another heart (not so good). Did East really think two heart tricks were cashing? Declarer ruffed, drew trumps and claimed.

What card(s) does East need to defeat four spades?

Do you see it? As little as the six, yes, the six of spades or higher. After cashing the ♡A, play a third club.

If West can ruff with the ♠6 or higher, dummy must overruff with the ♠A and East has a trump trick. That's not asking for a lot, is it?

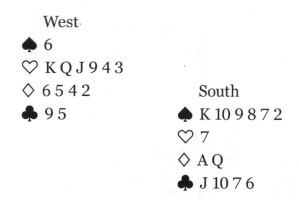

West
♠ 6
♡ K Q J 9 4 3
◇ 6 5 4 2
♣ 9 5

South
♠ K 10 9 8 7 2
♡ 7
◇ A Q
♣ J 10 7 6

DEAL # 76 SERIOUSLY?

				North
East	South	West	North	♠ 8 7 4 2
1♣	1♠	P	2♣	♡ A K J 9 6
3♣	3♠	P	4♠	◇ K Q
	All Pass			♣ 6 3

Opening Lead: ♣ 5

East
♠ A
♡ 7 4 3
◇ J 10 9
♣ A K J 10 9 8

East won Trick 1 with the ♣A and played the ♣K as West followed with the ♣4, declarer with the ♣2 and the ♣Q.

How should East continue the defense?

Afraid of a ruff/sluff, declarer obviously being void of clubs, East switched to the ◇J. Declarer won in dummy and played the ♡AK, discarding his last club. Declarer led a spade.

East won the ace perforce and now realized a ruff/sluff didn't matter. She led the ♣J, but declarer ruffed in hand high, drew the last trump and claimed.

"When did you think we switched to leading MUD," asked West?

Would you have been fooled by that falsecard? Seriously?

I would hope not. That would mean the opening lead was the 5 from 752.
All East needs is West to have a trump higher than the ♠8.

West
♠ 9 3
♡ Q 10 5 2
◇ 8 7 5 4 2
♣ 5 4

South
♠ K Q J 10 6 5
♡ 8
◇ A 6 3
♣ Q 7 2

DEAL # 77 KEEP TRYING

North	South	West	North	East
♠ J 6	1♠	2♢	3♣	P
♡ A Q 6	3♠	P	4♠	All Pass
♢ 9 3				

West

♠ A 8 2
♡ K J
♢ A K 8 7 4 2
♣ 7 2

♣ K Q J 10 4 3   Opening Lead: ♢Ace

At Trick 1, East follows with the ♢10.
West continues with the ♢K, East playing
the ♢5. West plays a third diamond, but declarer
ruffs with dummy's ♠J. East discards a low heart.
Declarer leads a spade to his king.

How should West continue?

Should West duck? If he wins the trick, then what? West won and shifted to a club.
Declarer won the ace in hand, drew trumps, and claimed.

Was it hopeless or could the defense have prevailed?

As usual, look to the trump suit. South has to have the ♣A from the bidding and
will take the heart finesse if he needs it. But check out those trump spots.

The eight in your hand is getting bigger. The ace, king, and jack are accounted for,
but if East has the nine or ten?

Play yet another diamond. This time partner ruffs with the ♠9, declarer overruffs
with the ten. You now have ♠82 behind declarer's ♠Q7.

I know you can take the setting trick.

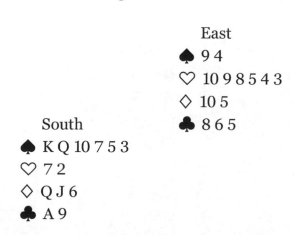

East

♠ 9 4
♡ 10 9 8 5 4 3
♢ 10 5
♣ 8 6 5

South

♠ K Q 10 7 5 3
♡ 7 2
♢ Q J 6
♣ A 9

DEAL # 78 CAREFUL

East	South	West	North	North
2♡	2♠	4♡	4♠	♠ 10 7 3
	All	Pass		♡ 8

North
♠ 10 7 3
♡ 8
◇ A K J 10 6
♣ J 10 5 3

East
♠ 8 4
♡ A K 10 7 6 3
◇ 9 7 3 2
♣ 7

Opening Lead: ♡ 4

West led a heart to East's king. At Trick 2, East
returned the ♣7. Declarer played the king, West
the ace, then the queen and continued with the nine.
Declarer covered with dummy's jack.

How should East continue the defense?

East ruffed with the ♠4 and declarer overruffed with the ♠5. He played the
♠AK, drawing the outstanding trumps and claimed.

West did not look happy. "What?" asked East. "Did you want me to return a heart
instead of a club?"

If you are ruffing something, really ruff it!

If East ruffed with the ♠8, not the ♠4, South has to overruff with his ♠Q, not
his ♠5 and West scores a trick with his ♠J92 for the setting trick.

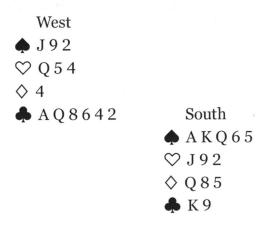

West
♠ J 9 2
♡ Q 5 4
◇ 4
♣ A Q 8 6 4 2

South
♠ A K Q 6 5
♡ J 9 2
◇ Q 8 5
♣ K 9

DEAL # 79 HIDDEN TRICK

North

♠ K Q
♡ 10 9 7
♢ A K J 10 7
♣ A K 10

North	South
1♢	2♠*
4♠	All Pass

• Weak Jump Shift

East

♠ A 4
♡ 8 6 5 3
♢ 8 4 3 2
♣ Q 7 4

Opening Lead: ♡ Ace

West led the ♡AK and a third heart, declarer playing the 4, J, & Q. Declarer led a spade to the dummy. How should East defend? Win or duck? If you win, then what?

East won the ♠A and returned a spade, hoping to score the ♣Q. Declarer won the trump return, cashed the ♣AK and ruffed a club. He drew the last trump and claimed.

Any other ideas? You know there must be a trump trick somewhere.

The thirteenth heart can promote a trump trick for partner's ♠10 if he has it, but cannot do so while dummy still has a trump to overruff West. So wait to win the ♠A until dummy's last high trump is gone, then lead your last heart.

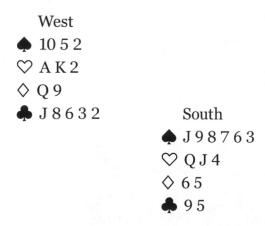

West

♠ 10 5 2
♡ A K 2
♢ Q 9
♣ J 8 6 3 2

South

♠ J 9 8 7 6 3
♡ Q J 4
♢ 6 5
♣ 9 5

When East returns the last heart, West has ♠ 10 behind declarer's ♠ J 9. Down one. Well done!

DEAL # 80 WAIT, WAIT, WAIT

North	South		North	
1♢	1♡		♠ 7	
2♣	2♠*		♡ Q J	
3♣	3♡		♢ K Q J 5 4	East
4♡	6♡		♣ K J 6 5 4	♠ 8 3

All   Pass

• Fourth Suit Forcing, often artificial   ♡ K 8 3

Opening   Lead: ♠ Queen   ♢ 10 7 6 2

                                              ♣ Q 10 3 2

The opening lead marked declarer with the ♠AK. South won Trick 1 with the ace and ruffed a spade with the ♡J. East has a sure trump trick now. Declarer led the ♢K and ruffed it. South next led another spade and ruffed with the ♡Q.

How should East defend? If he overruffs, what should he return?

East overruffed and tried to shorten declarer with another diamond. Declarer ruffed, drew the last trumps with the ♡A10 and claimed.

"A little patience partner, please," said West. "What was the hurry?"

Was West right? If East can just keep his finger off that heart king another moment, something good is about to happen. Remember don't overruff with natural trump tricks; a discard often promotes a second trump trick.

                West
                ♠ Q J 10 9 4 2
                ♡ 9
                ♢ A 9 8 3   South
                ♣ 9 7   ♠ A K 6 5
                                      ♡ A 10 7 6 5 4 2
                                      ♢ void
                                      ♣ A 8

If East does not overruff, declarer has ♡A10. Since West has the ♡9, East's ♡K83 is about to take two tricks.

DEAL # 81 IT'S A GUESS

				North
East	South	West	North	♠ 9 7 4 2
1♠	4♡	All	Pass	♡ J
				◇ K J 8

Opening Lead: ♠ 5

North
♠ 9 7 4 2
♡ J
◇ K J 8   East
♣ K Q J 7 6   ♠ A K 8 6 3
                          ♡ A
At Trick 1, East wins the ♠K, as   ◇ 7 6 3
declarer drops the jack.   ♣ A 10 9 4
How should East continue?

Had West led a singleton spade or was the lead from ♠Q105? Sometimes in bridge, besides good play, good guessing is required too.

Or finding a way to avoid guessing. East returned the ♠3, suit preference for clubs, hoping West could ruff.

Declarer ruffed, knocked out the aces of hearts and clubs and made four hearts.

Was there any way to avoid the guesswork?

East's other option at Trick 2 is West might be leading from ♠Q105, but have a doubleton club. Cash the ♣A and see West's card. If she plays a high card, continue clubs and more clubs after winning the trump ace. If West plays a low club, try for the spade ruff. (But it's still a bit of a guess. Both West and South may play low clubs under the ♣A. You can't be sure.)

West
♠ Q 10 5
♡ 10 6 3
◇ 10 9 5 4 2   South
♣ 8 3   ♠ J
                    ♡ K Q 9 8 7 5 4 2
                    ◇ A Q
                    ♣ 5 2

At Trick 2, West will play the ♣8. On the third round of clubs, West will uppercut declarer with the ♡10. Down one.

83

DEAL # 82 NO UPPERCUT, BUT…

		South	North
	North		
	♠ 6 5 3	1♠	2♠
	♡ K Q 8	3♡ ^	4♠
	◇ 5 4 2		
West	♣ Q 6 3 2	All Pass	
♠ 8 4		^ Help suit game try	
♡ 6 5		Opening Lead: ◇ Ace	
◇ A K 7			
♣ J 10 8 7 5 4			

West continues with the ◇K and a third diamond to East's queen, declarer following three times. East continues with a fourth diamond, declarer ruffs with the ♠9. How should West continue?

East was trying for a trump promotion, hoping West could ruff higher. Declarer plays a heart to dummy and a trump to his queen. He plays another heart to dummy and repeats the trump finesse. Declarer claims.

Could the defense have prevailed?

Perhaps. The try for an uppercut failed. What did you discard at Trick 4 when you could not overruff?

If you discarded a heart, plus 100. If you discarded a club, minus 620. South can't reach dummy twice if you discarded a heart; you will ruff.

	East
	♠ K 7 2
	♡ 4 3 2
South	◇ Q J 10 8
♠ A Q J 10 9	♣ A K 9
♡ A J 10 9 7	
◇ 9 6 3	
♣ void	

DEAL # 83 OPENING LEAD?

West	South	West	North	East
♠ A K 9 7 3	1♡	1♠	2♣	P
♡ J 8 3	3♣	P	3♠	Dbl
◇ K J 6 4	P	P	ReDbl	P
♣ 5	4♣	P	4♡	All Pass

West is on lead after a long auction to 4♡. What should he lead?

West led the ♠ Ace. Do you agree? Any other choices?

What should be the meaning of East's double? She passed over 2♣ so she doesn't have a spade raise. This double should only be to help West with the lead, and should show one of the top honors, saying it's OK to lead a spade.

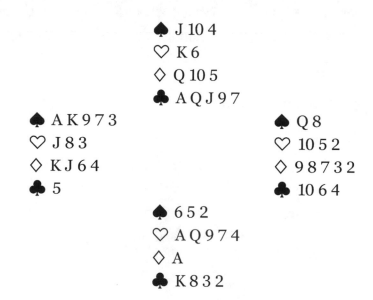

With the opening lead of the ♠AK and a third spade, East gets a ruff. Declarer has the rest.

With the opening lead of a low spade and a spade return, after three rounds of spades, another spade lets East ruff with the ♡10, promoting a trump trick for West, the setting trick.

DEAL # 84 ENCOURAGE WHAT?

North
♠ 10 5 4
♡ A 6 5 4
◇ J 4
♣ A K J 7

North	East	South	West
1♣	1♠	2♡	P
3♡	P	4♡	All Pass

West
♠ 7 2
♡ K 9 8
◇ K 10 9 8 2
♣ 9 6 4

Opening Lead: ♠ 7

East won Trick 1 with the ♠Q, and cashed the ♠AK, the declarer following. What should East discard at Trick 3? How should the defense continue?

East discarded an encouraging ◇10 at Trick 3. East switched to a diamond. Declarer won the ace and led the ♡Q. West ducked. Declarer continued with the ♡J. Declarer's trumps were ♡QJ1072. His diamond loser was discarded on the long club.

Making four hearts.

Any suggestions? What might you discard at Trick 3 to improve the defense?

East
♠ A K Q 6 3
♡ 3
◇ 7 6 5 3
♣ 8 5 3

South
♠ J 9 8
♡ Q J 10 7 2
◇ A Q
♣ Q 10 2

West does better to try for a trump promotion. Discard the ◇2. If East continues another spade, declarer has no winning options. If he ruffs low in hand, West's overruff forces dummy's ace.

If declarer ruffs high, West can discard and will make a trump trick later.

DEAL # 85 AVOIDING THE UPPERCUT

♠ 8 6 5 4
♡ 7 2
♦ A K
♣ A Q J 10 7

♠ K Q 10 9 3
♡ Q J 6
♦ J 10 6
♣ K 8

South opened 1♠ and North bid 2NT, a forcing spade raise. South bid 4♠, a minimum with no shortness. West led the ♡ 10.

East won the ♡K, cashed the ♡A, and played a third heart. West followed.
If you can hold your trump losers to one, you are bringing this home. How should you continue?

Cross to dummy, either ruffing this third heart trick (nothing to discard) or a diamond and lead a spade. East wins the ♠A, West follows with a small spade, and East plays another heart. Darn!

Now what? Ruff with the ♠10 and get overruffed or ruff with the ♠Q and cash the ♠K, hoping for 2-2 spades?

I don't know. Who was East? Sneaky enough to be giving you a losing option when she held ♠AJ7 and knew if she played low on the first spade, you could not go wrong? If she had singleton ace, you cannot make the hand; West started with ♠J72. If spades are 2-2, you have to guess.

Tough game. The point of the hand is from East's perspective with ♠AJ7 of giving declarer a losing option when game was cold.

East's Hand: ♠ A J 7 ♡ A K 5 4 3 ♦ Q 7 4 ♣ 9 5

DEAL # 86 TRUMP MANAGEMENT

♠ A K 10 7 5
♡ 6 3
◇ A K 8
♣ 9 4 2

♠ J 2
♡ K Q J 10 5 4
◇ Q J 6
♣ J 6

North opened 1♠ and East overcalled 2♣. South bid 2♡, forcing for one round. North liked his hand and bid 3◇ rather than a non-forcing 2♠.

South bid 4♡. West led the ♣ 3. Plan the play.

East won Trick 1 with the ♣Q and continued with the ♣A. West followed with the five. When East led the ♣K, South ruffed as West followed.

Declarer led the ♡K, East won the ace and played another club. Now what?

Declarer ruffed high and led the ♡Q. When East showed out, declarer was down one, losing a trump trick to West.

The only danger was 4-1 trumps. East almost surely has the ♡A. If declarer starts trumps from the dummy, he can avoid this danger. Then he can afford to ruff the club continuation high.

West	East
♠ 9 8 6	♠ Q 4 3
♡ 9 8 7 2	♡ A
◇ 10 7 3	◇ 9 5 4 2
♣ 10 5 3	♣ A K Q 8 7

DEAL # 87 AVOIDING THE TRUMP PROMOTION

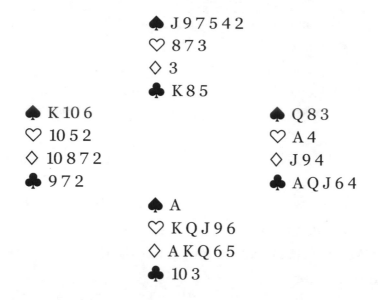

♠ J 9 7 5 4 2
♡ 8 7 3
♢ 3
♣ K 8 5

♠ K 10 6
♡ 10 5 2
♢ 10 8 7 2
♣ 9 7 2

♠ Q 8 3
♡ A 4
♢ J 9 4
♣ A Q J 6 4

♠ A
♡ K Q J 9 6
♢ A K Q 6 5
♣ 10 3

South opened 1♡ and North bid 1♠, planning on taking a 'preference' to hearts. East bid 2♣, South bid 3♢. When North bid 3♡, South bid 4♡.
West led the ♣ 2.

Trick 1 went ♣ 2; 5, J, 3. East continued with the ♣A and another club. Declarer discarded a diamond as West followed.

Declarer played a trump to his king which won. He now had to guess; had East started with ♡Ax or Axx? Declarer led the ♡Q. East won and played another club, promoting West's ♡10 into the setting trick.

Could this guesswork have been avoided?

Yes with better timing. At Trick 4, declarer should led low to his ♡K. Then cash the ♢A and ruff a diamond. Now he can again lead a trump from dummy thru East.

East has no recourse. Whether he began with two or three, his ace captures air. No promotion, no harm.

DEAL # 88 TO COVER OR NOT TO COVER

	North	South	North
	♠ 9 8 7 6 3	1♡	1NT*
	♡ 8 3	3♠^	4♣
	◇ 10 9 6 2	4◇	6♡
West	♣ A K		All Pass

West
♠ A Q 4
♡ J
◇ J 8 7 4 3
♣ Q J 8 6

* Forcing, one round
^ Self splinter
Opening Lead: ♣ Queen

West led the ♣Q against 6♡. Declarer cashed the ♣AK and led a trump to his hand dropping West's jack. Declarer now led the ♣10.

How should West defend?

West covered the ♣10 with the ♣J and declarer ruffed. Declarer drew trumps and after losing a trick to the ♠A had twelve tricks: seven hearts, one ruff, three clubs, and one diamond.

Would you have covered? What piece of information was missing?

What card did East play at Trick 3? How many clubs does South have? You saw what happened when West covered. Since declarer has nothing to discard from dummy, he needs to ruff the ♣9. When East overruffs, declarer is down one.

East
♠ K J 10 2
♡ 9 6 5
◇ K Q 5
♣ 7 4 2

South
♠ 5
♡ A K Q 10 7 4 2
◇ A
♣ 10 9 5 3

DEAL # 89 COUNT TO FORTY

North
- ♠ Q 7 5
- ♡ J 10 8
- ◇ K 8
- ♣ A K 10 9 5

East
- ♠ J 10 8
- ♡ Q 9 6 4
- ◇ Q J 10 9
- ♣ J 2

South	North
1♠	2♣
2♠	4♠
All Pass	

Opening Lead: ♡ Ace

West led the ♡A and East played an encouraging nine. West continued with the ♡K and another heart to East's ♡Q, as declarer followed.

How should East continue?

Not wanting to give declarer a ruff/sluff, East shifted to the ◇Q. Declarer won the ace, drew trumps and claimed the rest.

Was this the best defense? How could East have known what to do?

Can you do some simple arithmetic? The dummy has 13 HCP. You, East, have 7, West has shown 7 at Tricks 1 and 2, and declarer opened the bidding so let's give him 13. Let's see, that's 40.

Where do you think you are going to score the setting trick?

Ruff/sluff- sluff what? Which winner?

Another trick can only come from the trump suit. Play the thirteenth heart. When West ruffs with the ♠9, you have the setting trick in trumps.

West:
- ♠ 9
- ♡ A K 5
- ◇ 7 6 5 4 3 2
- ♣ 8 7 4

South
- ♠ A K 6 4 3 2
- ♡ 7 3 2
- ◇ A
- ♣ Q 6 3

DEAL # 90 LET DECLARER GUESS?

	North		North	South
	♠ K 5 2		1♣	1♡
	♡ K J 7 4		4◇^	4♡
	◇ A			All Pass
	♣ A K J 8 3		^ Splinter heart raise	

West
♠ Q J 10 7 4
♡ A 3
◇ 4 3
♣ 10 9 4 2

Opening Lead: ♠ Queen

The ♠Q held the first trick. West continued with the ♠J winning, and declarer ruffed the third spade. Declarer now led a small trump. How should West continue the defense?

West played low and after a bit of thought, declarer played the king from dummy. A second heart from dummy dropped East's ♡Q and West's ♡A.

Declarer claimed.

Good guess by declarer or could the defense have done better?

There is no advantage for West to duck the first heart. If West wins the ♡A and plays a fourth spade. declarer has no winning options. East scores his ♡Q.

East
♠ A 8 6
♡ Q 10
◇ J 8 7 6 5 2
♣ 7 6

South
♠ 9 3
♡ 9 8 6 5 2
◇ K Q 10 9
♣ Q 5

Thanks to Frank Stewart for this theme.

Printed in the United States
by Baker & Taylor Publisher Services